Ode to Mysticism
玄機賦

an English translation with commentaries

by
Hung Hin Cheong

Ode to Mysticism
玄機賦

Published in Kuala Lumpur, Malaysia by JY Books Sdn. Bhd. (659134-T)

Text © Hung Hin Cheong 2011
Design and illustrations © JY Books Sdn. Bhd.

First Edition July 2011

The author's moral rights have been asserted. All rights reserved worldwide. No part of this book may be copied, used, subsumed, or exploited in fact, field of thought or general idea, by any other authors or persons, or be stored in a retrieval system, transmitted or reproduced in any way, including but not limited to digital copying and printing in any form whatsoever worldwide without the prior agreement and written permission of the publisher.

Quantity discounts of JY Books titles are available for educational, business or sales promotional use. For information, please contact:

JY Books Sdn. Bhd. (659134-T)
19-3, The Boulevard, Mid Valley City, 59200 Kuala Lumpur, Malaysia.
Tel : +603-2284 8080 | Fax : +603-2284 1218 | Email : info@jy-books.com

DISCLAIMER:

The publisher JY Books Sdn Bhd and the author, Hung Hin Cheong, have made their best efforts to produce this high quality, informative and helpful book. They have verified the technical accuracy of the information and contents of this book. Any information pertaining to the events, occurrences, dates and other details relating to the person or persons, dead or alive, and to the companies have been verified to the best of their abilities based on information obtained or extracted from various websites, newspaper clippings and other public media. However, they make no representation or warranties of any kind with regard to the contents of this book and accept no liability of any kind for any losses or damages caused or alleged to be caused directly or indirectly from using the information contained herein.

Table of Contents

Foreword by Joey Yap	v
Introduction	vii

Part-1: (*xuan kong* version)		
Chapter 1.1:	In Principle…	3
Chapter 1.2:	"Growth" & "Co-prosperous" Interactions	17
Chapter 1.3:	"Control" (Clash) Interactions	41
Chapter 1.4:	Health Issues	49
Chapter 1.5:	Glad Tidings	53
Chapter 1.6:	And So On…	61

Part-2: (8-Mansions version)		
Chapter 2.1:	Stars & Palaces	69
Chapter 2.2:	East Group West Group	83
Chapter 2.3:	Negative Stars	101
Chapter 2.4:	Defective Palaces	107
Chapter 2.5:	Landform Blessings	111
Chapter 2.6:	Body Parts	117
Chapter 2.7:	East/West Differences	119

Appendices:		
Appendix-1:	"Wandering Stars"	125
Appendix-2:	"Star-Palace Interaction"	131
Appendix-3:	"Swinging Hexagrams"	145

Bibliography	87
About the Author	88

Foreword
by Joey Yap

It gives me great pleasure to write the foreword to **Ode to Mysticism**.

Hung Hin Cheong, the author behind both Xuan Kong Purple White Script (2009) and Secrets of Xuan Kong (2011), has gone to great lengths to translate the classical "Four Celebrated Poems of Xuan Kong" for the modern audience. It is difficult enough to decipher the text in its original ancient Chinese form and so translating it to modern English is by no means an easy task!

I consider Mr Hung to be one of my most accomplished students and his commitment, passion and unmatched comprehension of Xuan Kong Feng Shui shines through in this work. The commentary found herein is insightful and will add a lot to the readers understanding of the topics at hand.

In the past fourteen years I have ran courses on various aspects of Chinese Metaphysics. Some of the many thousands of students I have taught have gone on to pursue a career educating others, passing on what they have learnt. Mr Hung has done just that and despite his limited free time – he is a successful businessman and full-time property investor - he has managed to put his passion for Chinese Metaphysics to use and authored this outstanding book, which contributes new information and understanding to the field.

Ode to Mysticism is a translation based on the classical texts, Xuan Ji Fu 玄機賦, by the legendary Song Dynasty (960 – 1279) Feng Shui master, *Wu Jing Luan* 吳景鸞.

It is, amongst the Four Poems, regarded as one of the seminal classics in discussing star combinations and interpretations in Xuan Kong Feng Shui, widely referenced and used by famous Qing Dynasty scholars namely *Shen Zhu Reng* 沈竹礽, *Tan Yang Wu* 談養吾 and *Kong Zhao Su* 孔昭蘇 of the late Qing/early Republic period.

The Four Poems of Xuan Kong include: Xuan Kong Mi Zhi 玄空秘旨 (Secrets of Xuan Kong), Fei Xing Fu 飛星賦 (Ode to Flying Stars), and Zi Bai Jue 紫白訣 (Purple White Scripts).

What many people are unaware of is that the text actually speaks of Eight Mansions Feng Shui! When I mentioned this to Mr Hung during a discussion over coffee, it ignited his interest. After all, the classic Xuan Kong system differs widely from Eight Mansions Feng Shui and Ode to Mysticism is regarded as a Xuan Kong classic! Being the fervent scholar and researcher that he is, he proceeded to begin his own research after hearing about this fascinating paradox.

Sometime after this initial spark of fascination, the book you have in front of you was completed.

Ode to Mysticism reveals the Xuan Kong Life Palace divination technique, as well as the little known secret to understanding the many Xuan Kong Hexagram combinations which allow a practitioner to predict outcomes and foresee the future. It also describes a very deep side of Xuan Kong Feng Shui which differs hugely from the typical Flying Stars technique employed by today's practitioners.

Much has been discussed about the origins or how Master Wu actually wrote this Ode to Mysticism. From our research, we know that Ode to Mysticism wasn't really written by him, but actually it was possibly extracted from an article called Original Essence Classic 元髓經, penned by an unknown author, which was affixed to the Song Dynasty classic called "Entering Earth Eye" 入地眼, a classical text on Landform Feng Shui. This is the book that I normally referenced a lot during our China Feng Shui Excursions and Landform Feng Shui classes, and it has served as a base research book for Mr Hung as well.

I applaud Mr Hung's efforts in creating this indispensable book, which is a must-read for the English-speaking Xuan Kong Feng Shui enthusiasts and students the world over.

In addition to your own study, it is recommended you seek the guidance of a qualified Xuan Kong master to help with the information in this book.

Warmest Regards,

Joey Yap
Founder of Mastery Academy of Chinese Metaphysics
July 2011

www.joeyyap.com
www.facebook.com/joeyyapFB

Introduction

This poem constitutes another cornerstone of the "4 Celebrated Poems of *xuan kong* (玄空四大名賦)". 2 of these 4: "Purple White Script (紫白訣)" and "Secrets of *xuan kong* (玄空秘旨)" have already been published by JY Books in the present series, and in this 3rd book, we shall turn our attention to another of the poems, "Ode to Mysticism (玄機賦)".

The poem is attributed to the Song Dynasty *fengshui* scholar Wu Jing Luan (吳景鸞) (circa 1040), who also authored "Secrets of *xuan kong*". One would have logically expected one poem to be an addendum or sequel to the other, but that is not the case. In fact, "Ode to Mysticism" bears a striking resemblance to another article named "Original Essence Classic (元髓經)" of unknown authorship.

"Original Essence" was appended to "Entering Earth Eye (入地眼)", which in turn was attributed to Gu Tuo (辜托) (circa 990), but the article itself was probably older. Wu could have read "Original Essence" and decided to rewrite it in a manner compatible with his other masterpiece, "Secrets of *xuan kong*".

There is another possibility. The "Ode to Mysticism" can in fact be interpreted in the language of "8-Mansions" *fengshui*. Some scholars are of the opinion that the ode was a trick by Wu Jing Luan (吳景鸞) to secretly promote "8-Mansions" whilst making it look like a *xuan kong* poem. Now that is a very interesting and rather mischievous suggestion indeed, for *xuan kong* masters have traditionally turned their noses up at "8-Mansions". However, the idea may not be too farfetched, as there are indicators in Master Wu's writings that the man was something of a maverick.

In Part-1 of this book, I have interpreted the "Ode to Mysticism" from the *xuan kong* perspective; and in Part-2, reinterpreted it the "8-Mansions" way.

As far as I am aware, no other book, in Chinese or English, has done this. The twin approaches are offered to encourage a critical no-holds-barred study of classical *fengshui*. In the old days, that would have been considered heresy, and the protagonist unceremoniously kicked out of his school.

As with all ancient classics, the original text was devoid of paragraphs and punctuation marks. The line numbers and punctuations herein are later additions. The division into chapters and the chapter titles are entirely arbitrary.

The translation is not ad verbatim, but by and large I believe the flavour of the original text has been captured.

The text made reference to several idioms and allegories. I decided to relate these stories, in sidebars, to spice up an otherwise rather austere discussion.

Master Joey Yap's consent to write a foreword for this book is deeply appreciated. His contribution to the English speaking world of Chinese Metaphysics is unmatched by any other teacher and author; and his decision to feature "Ode to Mysticism" in one of his advanced *xuan kong* programs underscores the importance of this poem in the catalogue of *xuan kong* classics.

from the ramblings of one hhc, a fengshui crazee
Jun-2011

"Ode to Mysticism (玄機賦)"
the xuan kong Interpretation

PART-1
"Ode to Mysticism (玄機賦)"
the *xuan kong* Interpretation

Chapter 1.1
In Principle...

Chapter 1.1
In Principle…

OM01: 大哉！居乎成敗所係；危哉！葬也興廢攸關。

Grossly so! [In America they'd have said "Great Guns"!] **Success or failure is dependent on the house. Gravely so!** ["Smoking Guns"?] **Ascendance or futility is determined by burial.**

The poem starts off by reminding the reader that whereas the *fengshui* of a house affects the residents' success or failure in life, it is the *fengshui* of the burial ground that will affect the fate of the future generations, whether they will thrive or decline.

In *fengshui* terminology, a house for the living is called "*yang* dwelling (陽宅)", and a tomb is called "*yin* dwelling (陰宅)". Both need to abide by good *fengshui* principles, and essentially the same *fengshui* principles will apply to both *yang* and *yin* dwellings.

Chapter 1.1: In Principle...

> **OM02:** 氣口司一宅之樞，龍穴樂三吉之輔。
>
> The *qi* mouth serves as the pivot of the house. The meridian spot desires the support of the 3 Auspicious.

The primary "*qi* mouth (氣口)" of a house is its main door. As the residents move through this door, they carry the *qi* of the environment into the house. The main door constitutes one of 3 key features of a house that need to be assessed. The other 2 are the bed and the stove.

The back door, other secondary doors and even large windows are also *qi* mouths of sorts, but they are of less importance than the main door.

The second part of the line talks about "meridian spot (龍穴)". Strictly speaking, a "meridian spot" is the one point in an area where the concentration of *qi* is strongest. However, the term has also been used loosely to describe a burial pit. When we read Lines OM01 and OM02 together, it looks like the term simply means a grave in this case.

The second part of Line OM02 says a grave would benefit from the "3 Auspicious (三吉)". What are they? There are 2 interpretations:

➢ "3 Auspicious" refers to Stars-1, 6 and 8. We may think of them as "White Knights" [they are assigned the colour white in the gamut of colours for the 9 Stars]. These Stars are generally beneficial. Even when they are out of timing, they are at most incapacitated and frustrated but never belligerent;

➢ "3 Auspicious" refers to the current prosperous Star and the 2 future prosperous Stars. In Period-8, that would be Stars-8, 9 and 1.

In other words, if *xuan kong* Flying Stars are used to design a tomb, the Sitting and Facing of the tomb should also have timely Stars, or Stars-1, 6, 8.

Herein lies the problem: whereas for a house, the residents may be prepared to make adjustments in future when the Period changes, surely the same should not be required of a tomb? ☹

In fact, we do not normally use *xuan kong* Flying Stars for tomb alignment these days, but in principle it can be done. And remember, this is a *xuan kong* poem.

Chapter 1.1: In Principle...

> **OM03:** 陰陽雖云四路，宗支只有兩家。
>
> Although it is said there are 4 paths to *yin* and *yang*, at the source there are only 2 streams.

This line attracted several interpretations. In the *xuan kong* context, I find the following most credible:

"4 paths" refers to the 4 "Plates" of a *xuan kong* Flying Stars chart: "Earth Plate (地盤)" which displays the *luo shu* Stars; "Heaven Plate (天盤)" which displays the Period Stars; "Sitting Plate (山盤)" which displays the Sitting Stars; and "Facing Plate (向盤)" which displays the Facing Stars.

"at the source… 2 streams" refers to the *yin* or *yang* polarity of the Sitting and Facing Mountains. The polarity may or may not change when the Period changes. *yin* polarity will cause the Stars to fly in a reverse order, whereas *yang* polarity will cause the Stars to fly forward.

[Please refer to the author's book "Secrets of *xuan kong*" Chapter 1 for a more detailed explanation.]

A reverse flight path will deliver the prosperous Star to the required palace. If the prosperous Sitting Star lands at the Sitting palace, we call it "Prosperous Sitting (旺山)"; and if the prosperous Facing Star lands at the Facing palace, we call it "Prosperous Facing (旺向)". These are desirable outcomes.

On the other hand, a forward flight path will deliver the prosperous Star to the palace diametrically opposite. If the prosperous Facing Star lands at the Sitting palace, we call it "Up Mountain (上山)"; and if the prosperous Sitting Star lands at the Facing palace, we call it "Down Water (下水)". These are undesirable outcomes.

Hence "reverse flight" or "forward flight" makes all the difference between a desirable chart and an undesirable one. Line OM03 may be paraphrased to say "there may be 4 sets of Stars (*luo shu*, Period, Sitting and Facing) in a chart, but ultimately it's only *yin* flight or *yang* flight that makes the key difference.

Chapter 1.1: In Principle...

> **OM04:** 數列五行，體用恩仇始見。
>
> There are 5 Metaphysical elements. Their "Body" and "Application" will reveal the benefactor and enemy.

The 5 Metaphysical elements are of course Wood, Fire, Earth, Metal and Water. A student of Chinese Metaphysics must be thoroughly familiar with the "growth" and "control" (clash) cycles of these 5 elements.

"Body (體) and Application (用)" is a difficult concept. Almost every *fengshui* classic talks about "Body" and "Application", but not one has bothered to provide a comprehensive definition thereof. One of the most popular, and useless, statements is that "Early Heaven becomes the Body, Later Heaven becomes the Application (先天爲體，後天爲用)". So?

Neither am I so bold as to attempt a comprehensive definition. All I can offer is that in the present context, "Body" refers to the intrinsic relationship between 2 elements: say, the beneficial relationships of Wood (Star-3, 4) growing Fire (Star-9); Fire growing Earth (Star-2, 8); etc. On the other hand, there are the detrimental relationships of Wood (Star-3, 4) being controlled by Metal (Star-6, 7); Metal being controlled by Fire; etc. As these elemental relationships form the very core of *xuan kong* deliberations, they are regarded as a "Body" entity.

Then there is the *xuan kong* concept of timeliness. Star-3 progresses from rising to prosperous in Periods-1, 2 and 3. We say the Star is timely. After Period-3, Star-3 begins its decline and degenerates from weakness to belligerence. The state of a Star according to its timeliness is a qualifying factor rather than a basic character. It is therefore regarded as an "Application" entity.

For example, the Star conjunction 3-9 in Periods-1, 2 & 3 would be seen as prosperous Wood (Star-3) growing Fire (Star-9). Star-9 will stand to benefit from being grown by prosperous Star-3. As Wood growing Fire relates to brilliance, one can predict that the household will have intelligent and creative people.

Conversely, if the same Star conjunction 3-9 is seen in Periods-4, the ability of the weak Wood to grow Fire is questionable. Hence a prediction of intelligence would probably not be valid.

Another example: a Star conjunction 3-7 in Period-3 cannot be said to represent Metal (Star-7) hurting Wood (Star-3), as Star-3 is prosperous and cannot be hurt easily. Come Period-7 when Metal is strong and Wood is weak, it will be a different story.

Chapter 1.1: In Principle...

In other words, "Application" will always qualify "Body". We can draw an analogy from baking a cake. The dough made from flour, eggs and butter forms the "Body", while the flavouring and embellishments form the "Application". The dough makes it a cake, but it's the other stuff that makes the cake unique.

The term "benefactor and enemy" is simply another way of saying "auspicious and inauspicious", "beneficial and detrimental", etc., which is of course what *xuan kong* prediction is all about.

Line OM04 therefore says that we need to look into the timeliness of the Stars before we can ascertain whether a particular elemental relationship, expressed as a Star conjunction, is beneficial or otherwise.

This in fact is a fundamental premise of *xuan kong* Flying Stars. It can even be said that *xuan kong* places more emphasis on timeliness ("Application") than elemental relationships ("Body").

Chapter 1.1: In Principle...

> **OM05:** 星分九曜，吉凶悔吝斯彰。
>
> There are 9 different Stars. Their beneficial or detrimental status will make clear whether the outcome is regretful or precious.

This line merely echoes Line OM04 above, with which it forms a couplet (2-line poem), and further stresses the role played by the 9 Stars in determining the outcome of a given situation.

Each of the 9 Stars has its own attributes, but these attributes take on different expressions depending on whether the Star is timely or otherwise.

For example, a timely Star-1 stands for intelligence and high status, but that attribute turns to drink (or drug abuse in our present society) and wanton pleasure seeking when the Star falls out-of-timing.

Similarly, Star-2 when timely stands for property wealth and magnanimity like that of Mother Earth; whereas the Star is a harbinger of sickness and the dark side when out-of-timing.

And so on… The attributes of the 9 Stars are usually covered in some detail at intermediate level *xuan kong* study programs.

Chapter 1.1: In Principle...

> **OM06:** 宅神不可損傷，用神最宜健旺。
>
> The "House God" should not be hurt. It is best for the "Useful God(s)" to be healthy and prosperous.

"House God" refers to the static House Star featured in the "Growth & Prosperous Chart (生旺圖)" discussed in the "Purple White Script (紫白訣)" Upper Scroll. [See Line PW101 of my book "xuan kong Purple White Script" in the same series.]

In short, the static House Star is the *luo shu* Star at the Sitting of the property: i.e. Star-1 for a North Sitting property; Star-2 for a Southwest Sitting property; and so on. These Stars are static in the sense that they do not change with time.

Line OM06 says the "House God" should not be hurt, meaning any palace at which the House Star appears in a chart should not be threatened by negative landforms such as a deformed mountain, "Reverse Bow" water, etc. That is irrespective of whether the Star appears as a *luo shu* Star, Period Star, Sitting Star or Facing Star. The reasoning is that this Star, in whatever guise, is connected with the property. Hurting that Star would invariably impact the property negatively in some respect or other.

The second part says it is best for the "Useful God(s)" to be healthy and prosperous. Now "Useful Gods" refers to the Sitting Star at the Sitting palace and Facing Star at the Facing palace. The *xuan kong* Flying Stars technique places great importance on these 2 Stars. To a large extent, they determine the goodness or otherwise of a chart.

What makes a Star "healthy and prosperous"? Clearly that would be the case if the Star is prosperous (eg. Star-8 in Period-8), correctly located, and supported by external landforms. In other words, the prosperous Sitting Star is located at the Sitting palace and the prosperous Facing Star is located at the Facing palace, and the Stars are duly supported. That would make the chart "Prosperous Sitting Prosperous Facing (旺山旺向)", which is of course the most desirable.

Note that the line says "it is best for…". It doesn't say this has to be the case,

Chapter 1.1: In Principle...

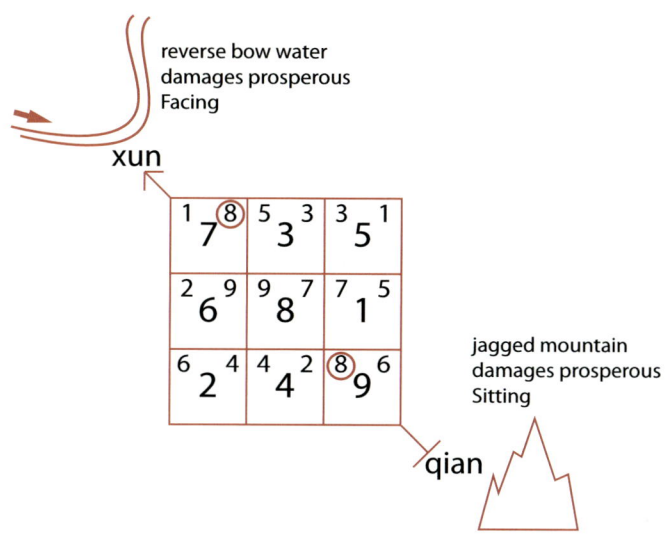

Fig-101: "Useful Gods" damaged

for other charts such as "Double Facing (雙星到向)", "Double Sitting (雙星到坐)" and "Up Mountain Down Water (上山下水)", though less desirable, are nevertheless usable.

Fig-101 illustrates a Period-8 property Sitting *qian* Facing *xun*. The chart is "Prosperous Sitting Prosperous Facing", and there is a mountain at the back and water in front. Can this property expect good people and wealth luck?

Unfortunately, the mountain at the back has jagged outcrops and the river in front takes the shape of a "Reverse Bow" cutting into the property. These negative landforms have totally negated the beneficial Stars. Such a property is in fact far worse than an "Up Mountain Down Water" chart that is not afflicted by such negative landforms.

Ode to Mysticism

Chapter 1.1: In Principle...

> **OM07:** 值難不傷，蓋因難歸閒地。
>
> If the presence of a disastrous entity does not inflict damage, it is because the disastrous entity resides at a passive location.

"disastrous entity" = negative Star

Many a time, the chart tells us that a property is susceptible to the ravages of a particular negative Star, but the residents report that nothing bad has happened. Such a situation deserves investigation. Often it is because the landscape outside the palace having that negative Star is serene and devoid of any negative landform or *sha qi* that could have unleashed the belligerence of the negative Star. Hence the negative Star remains passive.

In other words, a negative Star is only to be feared if it is provoked by *sha qi*, especially that emitted from negative landforms. *xuan kong* classics like "Secrets of xuan kong (玄空秘旨)" have taken pains to stress that virtual Stars, good or bad, must be corroborated by external landforms. Otherwise they are just numbers.

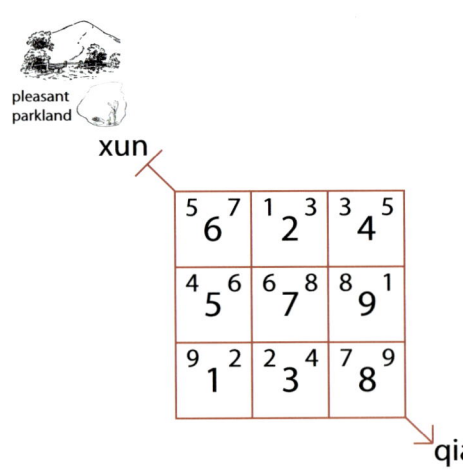

Fig-102: negative Star passive

Fig-102 shows a Period-7 property Sitting *xun* Facing *qian*. It is an "Up Mountain Down Water" chart. In addition, the Sitting Star at the Sitting palace is the much feared Star-5, which is out-of-timing in Period-7. According to the chart, the health of the residents should be an issue, especially for a middle-aged woman, the eldest daughter or a *gua*-4 person.

However, the residents reported they have stayed in this house for years, and everybody enjoyed good health.

On investigation, the *xun* palace of the property looks out onto a peaceful park with lush greenery and running water. There is no way Star-5 could have misbehaved in such an environment. This is an example of "disastrous entity residing at a passive location".

Chapter 1.1: In Principle...

> **OM08:** 逢恩不發，祇緣恩落仇宮。
>
> If one does not profit from meeting a benefactor, it is only because the benefactor has fallen into an enemy palace.

Line OM08 is the corollary of the previous line.

"benefactor"   =   positive Star

"enemy palace"   =   location where the positive Star is attacked by negative landforms, or otherwise disabled

Fig-103 shows a Period-7 property Sitting *you* Facing *mao*. It is a "Prosperous Sitting Prosperous Facing" chart. However, the prosperous Facing Star at *mao* does not see open space or water that it desires, but instead sees a jagged mountain. The household's hopes for wealth luck are completely dashed.

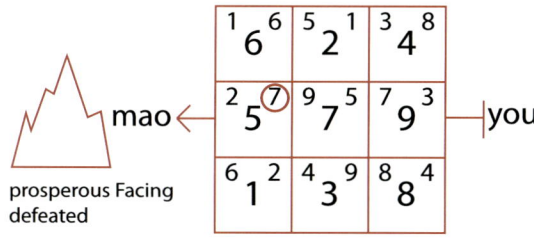

Fig-103: positive Star disabled

Ode to Mysticism   13

Chapter 1.1: In Principle...

> **OM09:** 一貴當權，諸凶懾服。
>
> One beneficial Star in power will cause multiple harmful entities to submit in fear.
>
> **OM10:** 眾凶剋主，獨力難支。
>
> If multiple harmful entities control the subject property, it will be difficult for a lone force to withstand the pressure.

The 2 lines appear contradictory, and need to be studied together.

"One beneficial Star in power" describes the prosperous Facing Star at the Facing palace, i.e. "Prosperous Facing", when we are addressing wealth prospects; and the prosperous Sitting Star at the Sitting palace, i.e. "Prosperous Sitting", when discussing people matters. Adequate support by the external landforms is of course mandatory.

Line OM09 says that with the prosperous Star at the right palace and supported, other harmful entities will be suppressed. The harmful entities may be negative Stars or negative landforms.

However, Line OM10 seems to have contradicted that statement. To make sense of both lines, a dose of interpretive judgment is needed.

For brevity, let us focus on "Prosperous Facing". The same will apply to "Prosperous Sitting" in respect of people matters. A "Prosperous Facing" is deemed strong enough to eclipse negative Stars at other less important palaces even though some of these negative Stars may be evoked by negative landforms outside.

On the other hand, if the "Prosperous Facing" is impaired by, say, inadequate landform support (inadequate but not damaging enough to negate completely) or the presence of multiple counteracting Stars at the Facing palace, then the prosperous Facing Star will be a lone force battling its adversaries. If, in addition, the subject property is attacked by serious landform "Killings" at other palaces, then we have the situation described in Line OM10.

Chapter 1.1: In Principle...

Of the *sha qi* or "Killings" that could affect a property, the following are some of the more serious:

➢   "Wind Gap (凹峰煞)" - a U-shaped gap in the encircling hills or buildings that will induce the wind to blow through the gap towards the area of the subject property;

➢   "Sky Crack Killing (天斬煞)" - a narrow gap between 2 tall buildings visible from the subject property;

➢   "Flying Blade (飛刀煞)" - the corner of a tall building nearby, like a blade of a sword threatening the subject property;

➢   A jagged or crumbling rock face (破碎砂), typically the remnants of quarrying, visible from the subject property;

➢   "Reverse Bow Water (反弓水)" - horseshoe shaped river or road with the convex side facing the subject property;

➢   "Spear Killing (槍煞)" - commonly called T-junction, pointing straight at a *qi* mouth of the subject property;

➢   "Pulling Nose Water (牽鼻水)": a straight drain or road leading downwards from the subject property in front of a *qi* mouth.

Then there are the modern man-made "Killings" like:

➢   High voltage power lines;

➢   Microwave transmission towers.

A question commonly asked is: how close must these "Killings" be for their negative *qi* to impact the subject property?

Regrettably there is no standard measure. My own rule-of-thumb [my engineering training is showing through here ☺] is that if the distance between the property and the offending object is more than twice the height of the property or the offending object, whichever is taller, then the impact is likely to be minimal.

More importantly, the offending object must not look menacing. If the sight of the object makes one feel uncomfortable, then no matter how far away, it is too near!

Ode to Mysticism

PART-1
"Ode to Mysticism (玄機賦)"
the xuan kong Interpretation

Chapter 1.2
"Growth" & "Co-prosperous" Interactions

Chapter 1.2
"Growth" & "Co-prosperous" Interactions

OM11: 火炎土燥，南離何益乎艮坤。

A hot fire scorches the earth. How would *li* at the South (Star-9) be able to benefit *gen* (Star-8) and *kun* (Star-2)?

The Fire of Star-9 grows the Earth of Star-2.

A "growth" interaction is normally considered beneficial, but Line OM11 herein points out this is not always the case. It says that if Fire is too intense, it will scorch the Earth instead. When is Fire too intense?

When Star-9 is untimely, Fire is weak. Surely a weak flame cannot be described as "hot fire"? More likely, "hot fire" refers to the presence a fire shaped landform outside *li* palace, such as a "Chastity" mountain, tall spire, electric pylon, television or microwave tower, temple, striking red building, etc. Alternatively, additional Fire Stars could fly into *li* palace to intensify the Fire. Do not forget that Star-9 is not the only Fire Star. Stars-2 & 7 are Early Heaven Fire Stars. Yet another possibility is the presence of Wood Stars (Stars-3, 4) at *li* palace to grow more Fire.

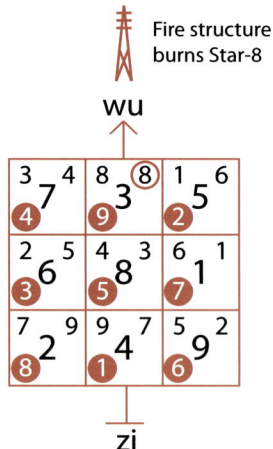

Fig-104: Fire scorches Earth

Fig-104 shows a Period-8 property Sitting *zi* Facing *wu*. The chart is "Double Facing" with 8-8 at the Facing palace. Elementary Flying Stars would recommend opening a door at *li* palace to make good use of Facing Star-8.

Chapter 1.2: "Growth" & "Co-prosperous" Interactions

However, if there is a Fire related object outside *li* palace, or when additional Fire Stars or Wood Stars fly in, then Star-8 will be scorched. Wealth opportunities will arise but will not deliver the desired results. Typical examples would be "burning one's fingers" in the stock market; or proceeds being locked in and inaccessible.

Also note that Fire is especially strong at *li* in this chart because the Period Star-3 (Wood) keeps feeding the Fire.

For this reason, at the higher *xuan kong* levels, we would prefer not to open a door at *li* for a Period-8 *wu* or *ding* facing house, if we have a choice.

In "Secrets of *xuan kong*" (Line SX76), it is stated that a conjunction of Stars-9, 8 & 2 signals accumulation of great wealth. That is provided the Stars are timely and supported. If Star-9 is afflicted, the wealth goes up in smoke, so to speak!

Chapter 1.2: "Growth" & "Co-prosperous" Interactions

> **OM12:**　水冷金寒，坎癸不滋乎乾兌。
>
> When water is cold and metal bitterly so, *gui* at *kan* (Star-1) will not be nourished by *qian* (Star-6) and *dui* (Star-7).

This line is the corollary of Line OM11. If Fire is too hot, it will scorch the Earth. Likewise, if Metal is too cold, it will freeze the Water rendering it useless.

When is Metal too cold? When the Metal Stars (6 & 7) are untimely and/or afflicted by negative landforms.

In other words, Star conjunctions 1-6, 1-7 are not always positive. Timeliness and landform support have to be taken into account.

The story is very different if Metal is not handicapped and in addition there is Earth present to grow more Metal. The situation is described in "Secrets of *xuan kong*" Line SX18, where the conjunction of Earth-Metal-Water Stars points to landed property wealth.

Chapter 1.2: "Growth" & "Co-prosperous" Interactions

OM13: 然四卦之互交，固取生旺。

Of the interactions within the 4 Plates, one should invariably select "growth" and "co-prosperous".

"4 Plates" refers to the 4 sets of numbers in a *xuan kong* Flying Stars chart, namely the "Earth Plate (地盤)" that displays the *luo shu* Stars; the "Heaven Plate (天盤)" that displays the Period Stars; the "Sitting Plate (山盤)" that displays the Sitting Stars; and the "Facing Plate (向盤)" that displays the Facing Stars.

In most Flying Stars charts, the "Earth Plate" is not displayed, as this is an unchanging entity and all *fengshui* practitioners, even newbies, are expected to know it by heart.

The first part of Line OM13 points to a very important *xuan kong* feature that many students tend to miss out. It tells us that all the 4 sets of numbers interact with one another, and that the Sitting and Facing Stars are not the only ones that form Star conjunctions.

At the entry level, students are taught to focus on the Sitting and Facing Stars. As we progress in our *xuan kong* studies, we learn that the other permutations of Stars also tell their own stories. Besides reading the Sitting-Facing Stars, we can also read Sitting-Period, Facing-Period, Sitting-*luo shu*, and Period-*luo shu*. In fact there are more possibilities if we take into account the Annual Star, Monthly Star, landform Star, etc. Indeed, sometimes 3-Star conjunctions tell yet another story. A taste of that is given in Lines OM11 and OM12 above.

The second part of Line OM13 says we should always look for "growth" or "co-prosperous" interactions, not only between Sitting and Facing Stars, but also the interactions between the other Stars. Any "growth" or "co-prosperous" interaction holds out the promise of positive outcome if used in the correct way.

Above all, this line offers us much greater freedom in planning the usage of the palaces in a given property. No longer are we constrained by the common Flying Stars rule that only the timely Facing Stars should be used for active functions (eg. door), and timely Sitting Stars for passive functions (eg. bedroom). The untimely Stars may also be put to good use if they form "growth" or "co-prosperous" relationships with other Stars in the same palace.

This new freedom does not give us a carte blanche to ignore the basic rule that timely is strong and untimely is weak. An untimely Star is remedied to some extent by another Star growing it, but it will never become as strong as a timely Star. Nevertheless, the added flexibility can come in useful at times.

Chapter 1.2: "Growth" & "Co-prosperous" Interactions

> **OM14:** 八宮的締合，自有假真。
>
> Of the Star combinations in the 8 palaces, some are real others are false.

The "8 palaces" are of course the 8 peripheral palaces of a chart. Why 8 and not 9? That's because the central palace is not exposed to external landforms.

A Star conjunction is said to be "real", or effective, if it is supported by the appropriate type of landform outside. It is "false", or ineffective, if the external landform is inappropriate.

Let's say there is a 1-4 conjunction at a particular palace and Star-1 is timely. If in addition there is a tall slim and elegant structure called a "Scholar's Brush (文筆)" outside that palace (traditionally a pagoda, or better still a natural slim mountain with a straight pointed tip), we can confidently predict that the household will produce academics or outstanding writers, administrators, etc.

On the other hand, if the external landform is a "Literary Arts Star (文曲星)" (mountain with wavy top), or a stagnant polluted pond, then overindulgence in drink and debauchery is the more likely outcome.

Chapter 1.2: "Growth" & "Co-prosperous" Interactions

> **OM15:** 地天爲泰，老陰之土生老陽。
>
> Earth and Heaven make up the "Unity" Hexagram. The Earth of "Old *yin*" (Star-2) grows (the Metal of) Old *yang*" (Star-6).

The "Unity (泰)" Hexagram is made up of the Trigrams *kun* stacked on top of *qian*, ☰.

In the present context, it simply refers a 6-2 or 2-6 conjunction. Strictly, 6-2 makes up the "Unity" Hexagram whereas 2-6 makes up the "Stagnation (否)" Hexagram, but in the poem "Ode to Mysticism", just like its sibling "Secrets of *xuan kong*", Hexagram names are used rather loosely without observing the order of the Stars. [See Appendix-3]

2-6 represents Earth growing Metal, i.e. a "growth" interaction. In addition, *kun* and *qian* make up a natural *yin-yang* pair. If either one of the Stars is timely and supported, the conjunction is highly beneficial.

[The same topic is discussed in "Secrets of *xuan kong*" Line SX86.]

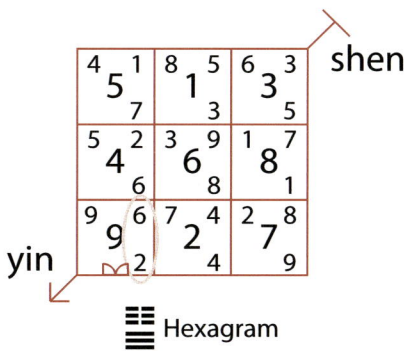

Fig-105: 2-6 conjunction

Fig-105 shows the chart of a Period-6 property Sitting *shen* Facing *yin*. The door at *gen* palace has the prosperous Facing Star. In the year 1983, the Annual Star-2 flew into *gen* palace, precipitating a 6-2 conjunction between the Facing Star and the Annual Star. The household should have experienced extraordinary wealth opportunities that year.

Ode to Mysticism

Chapter 1.2: "Growth" & "Co-prosperous" Interactions

Regrettably, as the conjunction involved the Annual Star, the opportunities would have only come by during that one year. Moreover, by the very next year, 1984, Period-6 has lapsed and Star-6 was no longer prosperous.

On the other hand, if Star-2 had come in the form of a "Huge Door (巨門)" mountain outside *gen* palace, then the household's good fortune would have lasted for the whole of Period-6.

[Note: Star-6 as the prosperous Facing Star requires open space out front to support it. Hence the "Huge Door" mountain should be some distance away, beyond a stretch of flat land outside *gen* palace.]

If the 6-2 conjunction involved the Sitting Star, it would have indicated people related happy events, like the birth of a child.

Chapter 1.2: "Growth" & "Co-prosperous" Interactions

> **OM16:** 若坤配兌女，庶妾難投寡母之歡心。
>
> If *kun* (Star-2) is matched with *dui* (Star-7), it is difficult for the subordinate wife to gain the widowed mother's approval.

In terms of elemental interaction, *kun* (Star-2) and *dui* (Star-7) also represent Earth growing Metal, but both Stars are *yin*. There is a saying that "*yang* on its own will not procreate; *yin* by itself will not sustain growth (孤陽不生，獨陰不長)". Hence the "growth" interaction is defective.

Line OM16 draws on the example of a strained relationship between the mother and the daughter-in-law, but a 2-7 conjunction covers much wider ground. It describes any conflict between the womenfolk where the age gap is wide. Naturally, the problem only crops up when the Stars are untimely and the external landforms are unfriendly.

If this Star conjunction occurs at an important location such as the main door, it also indicates a high chance of widowhood when Star-2 is untimely. Alternatively, the young women tend to be promiscuous when Star-7 is untimely. In any case, the males of the household are doomed to suffer a powerless or subservient existence.

Lines OM15 and OM16 remind us that for a "growth" relationship to be positive for procreation, the polarities must make up a *yin-yang* pair.

Chapter 1.2: "Growth" & "Co-prosperous" Interactions

> **OM17:** 澤山爲咸，少男之情屬少女。
>
> Marsh (Star-7) and Mountain (Star-8) make up the "Influence" hexagram. The young man's feelings belong to the young woman.

The "Influence (咸)" Hexagram is made up of the Trigrams *dui* stacked on top of *gen*, ☶.

As explained under Line OM15, the poem is not too bothered about the order of the Stars. Hence this line describes a 7-8 or 8-7 conjunction.

Like Line OM15 earlier, this line also describes an Earth growing Metal interaction between 2 polarity matching Stars. This is clearly a positive conjunction, promising great wealth. Of all the elemental interactions, Earth growing Metal represents wealth more than any other, provided of course the Stars are timely and supported.

Fig-106 shows 2 Period-7 charts: chart (a) Sitting *kun* Facing *gen*; chart (b) Sitting *ding* Facing *gui*. Both are "Double Facing" charts. Assuming that the door is located at the Facing palace and the external landforms are supportive in both cases, both properties should enjoy good wealth luck, but chart (a) has the added advantage of a 7-8 conjunction between the *luo shu* Star and the Facing Star at *gen*.

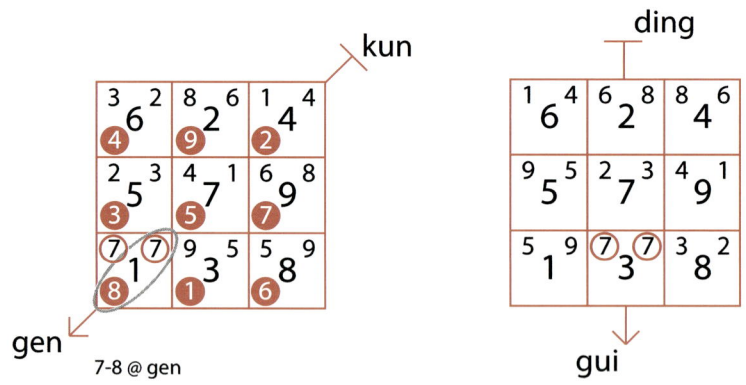

Fig-106: 7-8 conjunction

In terms of both syntax and semantics, Line OM17 is a natural follow-through from Line OM15, just as Line OM16 and Line OM18 make up a couplet. The author probably decided to interlace the 4 lines as a poetic variation.

Chapter 1.2: "Growth" & "Co-prosperous" Interactions

> **OM18:** 若艮配純陽，鰥夫豈有發生之機兆。
>
> If *gen* (Star-8) is matched with the pure *yang* (meaning *qian*, Star-6), like the widower, there will hardly be an opportunity to procreate.

This Line OM18 is in fact the response to Line OM16 in couplet style. What is said under Line OM16 about uni-polar interactions applies equally here. The Earth of Star-8 is supposed to grow the Metal of Star-6, but both Stars are *yang*. Hence the "growth" interaction is defective.

Having said that, Star-6 and Star-8 are both "White Stars" (White Knights) that are fundamentally benevolent. Their conjunction, especially in Period-6 when both Stars are timely, cannot be bad. It's just short of perfection.

For example, the conjunction could mean substantial wealth opportunities, but much hard work and undue stress have to be endured to realize the wealth.

As both Stars are *yang*, the conjunction also indicates women being disadvantaged. When the Stars are untimely, the wife's demise is a possibility.

Note that in a Period-7 property, the *luo shu* Star at *qian* palace is 6 and the Period Star is 8. There is therefore an intrinsic 6-8 conjunction at *qian*. Any Period-7 property having its door at *qian* will in fact risk male dominance to the detriment of the female.

This is also an example where conclusions can be drawn just by looking at the *luo shu* Stars and Period Stars, without even going into the Sitting and Facing Stars. This is what Line OM13 was driving at.

Ode to Mysticism

Chapter 1.2: "Growth" & "Co-prosperous" Interactions

> **OM19:** 乾兌託假鄰之誼；坤艮通偶爾之情。
>
> *qian* (Star-6) and *dui* (Star-7) make insincere neighbours. *kun* (Star-2) and *gen* (Star-8) are affectionate from time to time.

qian (Star-6) and *dui* (Star-7) are both Metal Stars. A "co-prosperous" interaction is normally regarded as beneficial, as the 2 Stars reinforce one another. However, a 6-7 conjunction has inherent flaws. Although Star-6 is *yang* and Star-7 is *yin*, the age gap is wide (old man and young girl). Moreover, Metal as an element is aggressive and competitive by nature. When both Stars-6 & 7 are timely, the conjunction is positive, but as soon as the Stars become untimely, we have an aggressive situation at hand.

A 6-7 conjunction is called "Cross Swords Killing (交劍殺)". It denotes conflict, robbery and the spilling of blood. Of course this only happens when the Stars are untimely and aggravated by negative landforms.

As *qian* and *dui* are neighbours on the *luo shu* chart, Line M19 describes their neighbourly relations as being insincere.

kun (Star-2) and *gen* (Star-8) are both Earth Stars. Unlike the Metal Stars, Earth Stars are not aggressive by nature. In spite of the age gap (old woman and young boy), 2-8 is not considered anti-social. [Oedipus complex is a Western issue. The Chinese would have regarded it as natural bonding, maybe a little overzealous, between a mother and her offspring ☺] Moreover, Earth and Earth will simply make more Earth. No conflict.

A 2-8 conjunction is usually beneficial. Line OM19 says the 2 Stars are affectionate from time to time. The renowned *xuan kong* master, Shen Zu Mian (沈祖綿), explained it this way:

In Periods-2, 5 & 8, properties facing the Trigram *kun* (made up of the Mountains *wei*, *kun* and *shen*) or the Trigram *gen* (made up of the Mountains *chou*, *gen* and *yin*) are particularly favourable. Properties Sitting *chou* Facing *wei*, or the other way around, will have a "Prosperous Sitting Prosperous Facing" chart. As for properties Sitting *gen/yin* Facing *kun/shen*, or the other way around, their charts will have a special structure called "Parent String Formation (父母三般卦)". In all these cases, Star-2 and Star-8 feature prominently at the Facing and Sitting palaces.

[Apart from the 4 standard *xuan kong* structures: "Prosperous Sitting Prosperous Facing", "Up Mountain Down Water", "Double Facing" and "Double Sitting", there are other special structures, one of which is the "Parent String Formation". These structures are usually explained in intermediate level Flying Stars books or study programs.]

Chapter 1.2: "Growth" & "Co-prosperous" Interactions

The 4 Period-8 charts that demonstrate the said features are shown in Fig-107. The student is encouraged to plot out the corresponding Period-2 and Period-5 charts for practice.

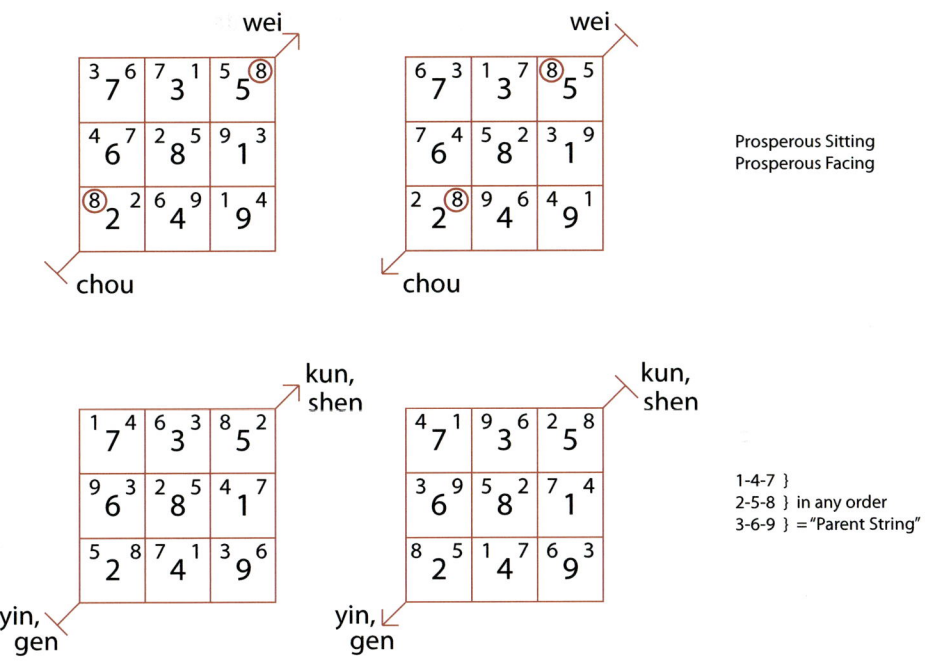

Prosperous Sitting
Prosperous Facing

1-4-7 }
2-5-8 } in any order
3-6-9 } = "Parent String"

Fig-107: Period-8 *kun/gen* (Trigrams) charts

Whether or not one buys Master Shen's explanation is unimportant. Just be aware that a 2-8 conjunction is usually beneficial. The worst that can happen is people opting to become monks and nuns. The possibility arises when the Stars are disabled, as explained in "Secrets of *xuan kong*" Line SX80.

Chapter 1.2: "Growth" & "Co-prosperous" Interactions

> **OM20:** 雙木成林，雷風相薄。
>
> A pair of wood becomes a forest. Thunder (Star-3) and Wind (Star-4) are mutually attracted.

Star-3 and Star-4 are the 2 Wood Stars. "Becomes a forest" implies a 3-4 conjunction.

The statement "Thunder and Wind are mutually attracted (雷風相薄)" is a line out of a poem that describes the universe in perfect balance.

[The classic "Speaking of Hexagrams (説卦傳)" says:

Heaven and Earth set the locations	天地定位
Mountain and Marsh pass the *qi* between them	山澤通氣
Thunder and Wind are mutually attracted	雷風相薄
Water and Fire do not shoot at each other	水火不相射

The verse describes the Early Heaven arrangement of the 8 Trigrams, which represents the universe in perfect balance.]

Frankly the statement is not helpful at all. In the first place, the real universe is far from perfect. Shen Zu Mian (沈祖綿) tried to explain that even in the Later Heaven arrangement of the 8 Trigrams, which represents the real imperfect universe, Thunder (*zhen*) and Wind (*xun*) are placed next to each other, and that in a way demonstrates mutual attraction. Be that as it may, I still do not see the relevance of that statement in the present context.

A 3-4 conjunction is a "co-prosperous" interaction. Stars-3 & 4 are also a natural *yin-yang* pair. Hence the conjunction should be benevolent. Indeed when the Stars are timely, the conjunction favours progeny and also indicates high social status. ["Secrets of *xuan kong*" Lines SX25, SX87]

However, there are hidden dangers. Unlike Metal, Wood is not overtly aggressive, but trees (Star-3) and herbaceous plants (Star-4) do fight for sunlight for their own survival in a forest. Then there are creepers and parasitical plants that exploit their hosts. The saying "it's a jungle out there" aptly describes the covert struggles in a forest.

Likewise, a 3-4 conjunction is a minefield of unseen trouble if the Stars are out-of-timing and aggravated by negative landforms. The conjunction points to manipulation, deception, fraud, embezzlement, and woman taking advantage of man. ["Secrets of *xuan kong*" Line SX87]

Chapter 1.2: "Growth" & "Co-prosperous" Interactions

> **OM21:** 中爻得配，水火方交。
>
> The middle line of the Trigrams forms a *yin yang* pair, which is why Water (Star-1) matches well with Fire (Star-9).

The symbol for the Trigram *kan* (Water, Star-1) is ☵; whereas that for *li* (Fire, Star-9) is ☲. The 2 Trigrams form a natural pair (2nd son and 2nd daughter).

Fig-108 compares the Early Heaven and Later Heaven arrangements of the 8 Trigrams.

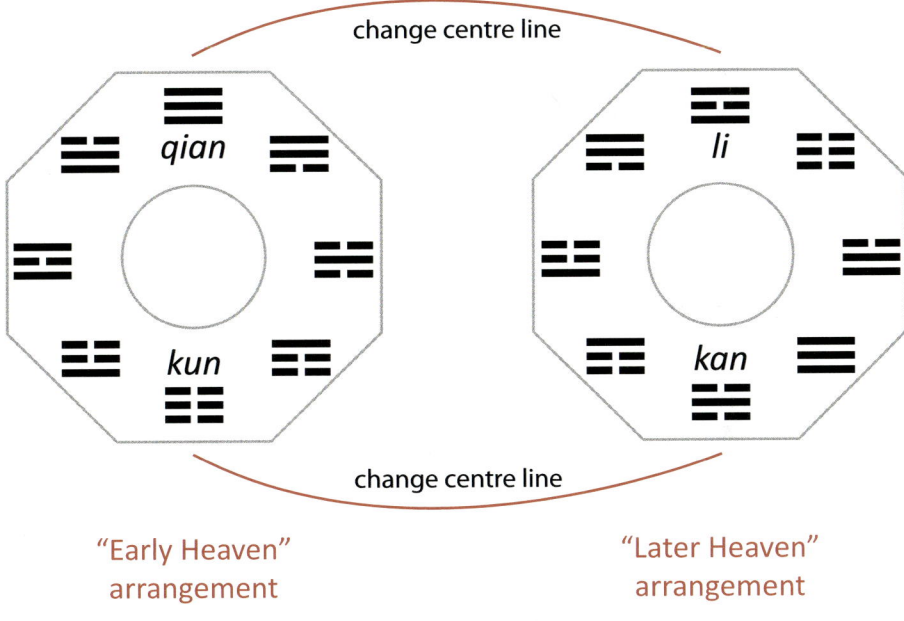

"Early Heaven" arrangement   "Later Heaven" arrangement

Fig-108: *li* & *kan*, *qian* & *kun*

First look at Later Heaven: li occupies the top position whereas kan occupies the bottom position. Now imagine that the middle lines of the 2 Trigrams are interchanged. li ☲ becomes *qian* ☰, and *kan* becomes *kun* ☷. Now look across at the Early Heaven diagram, isn't *qian* located at the top and *kun* at the bottom? The Trigrams *qian* and *kun* also form a natural pair (father and mother).

Ode to Mysticism

Chapter 1.2: "Growth" & "Co-prosperous" Interactions

This extraordinary match is the basis of the statement "Water and Fire do not shoot at each other (水火不相射)" in the poem describing the perfect universe (see Line OM20).

In the language of xuan kong Flying Stars, 1-9 is a "Later Heaven Combination" (commonly called "Combo-10"). It relates to wealth and other opportunities that are created by one's own efforts, provided of course that the combination is not defeated by negative landforms or unfortunate conjunctions of other Stars.

This positive view of a Water-Fire interaction is perhaps contrary to the notion that Water and Fire are supposedly adversarial (Water controls Fire). The Trigram story above dispels this notion. Water and Fire, in balanced amounts, are in fact mutually supportive.

In the real world, fire is required to thaw out water and water is used to regulate fire. Both heat (Fire) and water are necessary to sustain life on earth. Problems arise only when one overwhelms the other.

In terms of Hexagrams, 9-1 forms the "Accomplished (水火既濟)" Hexagram, with *kan* stacked over *li*. The Hexagram indicates a job well done. [The other way around with *li* over *kan*, the Hexagram actually becomes "Not Yet Accomplished (火水未濟)", which tells us the job is not done yet. However, as explained elsewhere in this book, the "Ode to Mysticism" does not pay too much attention to the order of the Stars, and both 1-9 and 9-1 are regarded positively.]

Chapter 1.2: "Growth" & "Co-prosperous" Interactions

> **OM22:** 木爲火神之本；水爲木氣之源。
>
> Wood enables Fire, just as Water is the source of Wood.

Wood grows Fire, and Water grows Wood.

This line serves as a prelude to the subsequent lines that deal with Wood-Fire and Water-Wood interactions.

Chapter 1.2: "Growth" & "Co-prosperous" Interactions

> **OM23:** 巽陰就離，風散則火易熄。
>
> *xun* (Star-4) and *li* (Star-9) are both *yin*. When the Wind scatters, the Fire is easily extinguished.

The Wood of Star-4 grows the Fire of Star-9, but both Stars are *yin*. Hence the "growth" interaction is flawed.

When either Star is timely, growth is deemed effective. 4-9 (Wood growing Fire) denotes intelligence. As both Stars are *yin*, one may predict that the brilliance is of a gentle and introspective nature, rather than brash and assertive.

When the Stars are out-of-timing or afflicted by negative landforms, the supposed "growth" is nullified. That is what is meant by the Wind putting out the Fire. The negative effects could be low intellect, lack of passion, relationship problems between women, lesbian tendencies, etc. As both Stars are *yin*, women tend to be impacted more than men.

Chapter 1.2: "Growth" & "Co-prosperous" Interactions

> **OM24:** 震陽生火，雷奮而火尤明。
>
> *zhen* (Star-3) is *yang* and grows Fire (Star-9). Thunder exerts itself and the Fire is especially bright.

The Wood of Star-3 grows the Fire of Star-9. It is *yang* Wood growing *yin* Fire, hence the required *yin-yang* balance is satisfied.

Wood growing Fire denotes intelligence. The difference between 3-9 and 4-9 is in the nature of the intelligence. Whereas 4-9 produces intelligent people who are contemplative and reflective, 3-9 produces the quick witted and expressive type - hence the description "... especially bright".

When the Stars are untimely or afflicted by negative landforms, constructive brilliance turns to impatience, aggressiveness and a perverse kind of street smartness.

Chapter 1.2: "Growth" & "Co-prosperous" Interactions

> **OM25:** 震與坎爲乍交；離共巽而暫合。
>
> *zhen* (Star-3) and *kan* (Star-1) make fickle acquaintances; *li* (Star-9) and *xun* (Star-4) form a temporary union.

The Water of Star-1 grows the Wood of Star-3, but both Stars are *yang*. Hence the "growth" interaction is flawed.

When the Stars are timely and supported, a 1-3 conjunction enhances humanity or wealth ["Secrets of *xuan kong*" Line SX79], but the *yang-yang* interaction is basically unstable. When the Stars turn untimely or are not supported by external landforms, then 1-3 produces petty people and trouble makers instead.

The second part of the line describes a 4-9 conjunction, which has already been discussed in Line OM23 earlier.

Chapter 1.2: "Growth" & "Co-prosperous" Interactions

> **OM26:** 坎元生氣，得巽木而附寵聯歡。
>
> *kan* (Star-1) is the source of vital energy. Obtaining *xun* Wood (Star-4) will bring about great celebrations.

This line describes the 1-4 Water grows Wood interaction.

Star-1 is *yang* and Star-4 is *yin*. Hence the "growth" is lasting, unlike 1-3 described in the previous line.

1-4 is traditionally associated with academic success, especially success in the public exams that were conducted to recruit scholars into the civil service (see sidebar).

This Star conjunction is discussed extensively in the "Purple White Script - Lower Scroll (紫白訣下篇)", and will not be repeated here.

It used to be one of the most sought after of Star conjunctions, before modern market oriented economics elevated the status of the businessman way ahead of the scholar or civil servant.

What if Stars-1 & 4 are out-of-timing and/or afflicted by negative landforms?

Another *xuan kong* classic "Ode to Flying Stars (飛星賦)" has this to say: "4 drifts and 1 becomes lustful (四蕩一淫)". I don't think there's a need to elaborate. [See "Ode to Flying Stars" Line FS22]

> *In feudal Chinese society, public exams were conducted periodically at district, provincial and national levels for the purpose of recruiting scholars into the civil service, and subsequently promoting them within the service.*
>
> *Of course this was not the only way to be admitted to the service. Buying a position was just as effective, and a lot quicker* ☺
>
> *Becoming a senior government official was a widespread aspiration as it represented a means to wealth and social status. The 1-4 star conjunction facilitated this pursuit.*
>
> *The modern equivalents would be academic excellence, and success in the literary and related fields.*

Chapter 1.2: "Growth" & "Co-prosperous" Interactions

OM27: 乾乏元神，用兌金而傍城借主。

If one is unable to benefit from the timeliness of *qian* (Star-6), making use of *dui* Metal (Star-7) is like a servant seeking employment from a master in a neighbouring city.

This line refers to Period-6 when Star-6 is prosperous and Star-7 is also timely. It says that if one is unable to use Star-6, be it as the Facing Star at the Facing palace or the Sitting Star at the Sitting palace, but one gets Star-7 instead, then it is almost as good as Star-6, for both Stars are Metal, and both are timely.

There are only 2 Period-6 charts that meet this condition. They are shown in Fig-109 herein. If Star-7 is supported by the external landforms, then the charts are as good as "Prosperous Sitting Prosperous Facing".

If we take a broader view, in Period-6 Star-7 is deemed as strong as Star-6 in whatever guise, whether *luo shu*, Period, Sitting, Facing, Annual, etc.

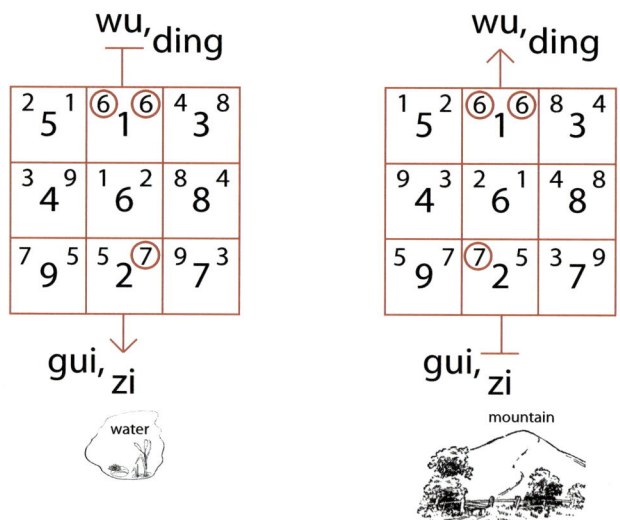

Fig-109: Star-7 in Period-6

Chapter 1.2: "Growth" & "Co-prosperous" Interactions

But does this apply in reverse during Period-7? The answer is "no". In Period-7, Star-6 is no longer timely. Line OM19 tells us *qian* and *dui* make insincere neighbours. When either Star is out-of-timing, the camaraderie is not sustainable.

The above is not the only explanation for Line OM27. For example, Shen Zu Mian (沈祖綿) explained the line in terms of the "Castle Gate Formula (城門訣)". With due respect, I remain skeptical.

Yet another explanation is that if there is no Earth around to grow the Metal of Star-6, then the presence of Star-7 will also help to strengthen Star-6. In other words, in the absence of a "growth" interaction, a "co-prosperous" interaction is also desirable. However, this statement is conditional upon both Stars being timely. [See Line OM19]

PART-1
"Ode to Mysticism (玄機賦)"
the xuan kong Interpretation

Chapter 1.3

"Control" (Clash) Interactions

Chapter 1.3
"Control" (Clash) Interactions

> **OM28:** 風行地上，決定傷脾。
>
> When Wind (Star-4) traverses the Earth (Star-2), the spleen will surely be hurt.

"Wind" = Star-4, Wood; "Earth" = Star-2, Earth.

Wood controls (clashes) Earth. Moreover both Stars are *yin*, - hence merciless.

A 2-4 conjunction indicates not only spleen ailments. Star-2 represents the abdomen and that includes the stomach, spleen and pancreas, as well as the digestive system, muscles, skin, female reproductive system, etc. Any of these body parts and functions can be affected when Star-2 is attacked.

Star-2 also represents the ultimate *yin*. Hence Star-2 in trouble could also precipitate depression, hallucinations, apparitions, haunting, and the like.

[Similar to Secrets of *xuan kong* Line SX64]

Chapter 1.3: "Control" (Clash) Interactions

OM29: 火照天門，必當吐血。

When Fire (Star-9) illuminates Heaven's Gate (Star-6), one will surely vomit blood.

"Fire" = Star-9; "Heaven's Gate" = *qian*, Star-6.

9-6 describes a Fire-Metal conflict, which is about the most violent of all the elemental conflicts.

As to why the vomiting of blood, the reasoning goes like this: the Trigram *qian* (Star-6) not only represents the head but also the lungs. Star-9 is red in colour. Traditionally the vomiting of blood is associated with tuberculosis and other lung ailments. Hence when Star-6 is damaged by Star-9, blood is vomited.

In fact, illnesses associated with the head, like migraine, meningitis, stroke, etc. are just as valid predictions.

Landforms that would aggravate the situation include jagged rock faces, power line, microwave transmission tower, tall spire, red building, etc.

Inside the house, the stove represents Fire. Hence locating the stove at the *qian* (Northwest) sector is not recommended, especially in Period-8, when the Period Star-9 flies to *qian*. Hence there is an inherent 6-9 conjunction at *qian* between the *luo shu* Star and the Period Star.

The family members likely to be impacted are the male head of household; an elderly man; or any *gua*-6 person.

[Similar to Secrets of *xuan kong* Line SX57]

Chapter 1.3: "Control" (Clash) Interactions

> **OM30:** 木見戌朝，莊生難免鼓盆之嘆。
>
> If Wood (in this case Star-4) faces *xu* (Star-6), it will be difficult to avoid the regrettable incident of Zhuang Sheng drumming on a basin. [Idiom meaning the demise of one's wife, see box]

The line describes a 4-6 conjunction, i.e. Wood-Metal conflict, when the Stars are untimely. The incident referred to is narrated in the box below.

> *The story of Zhuang Sheng drumming on a basin:*
>
> *Zhuang Sheng (莊生), better known as Zhuang Zi (369~286 BCE), was a famed Daoist philosopher cum poet cum sorcerer. He led a reclusive lifestyle, having turned down public office. His third marriage was to a beautiful and much younger woman by the surname Tian (田).*
>
> *Despite his wife's vehement declarations of undying faithfulness, Zhuang was not convinced. So he used sorcery to feign his own death, and turned up at his own wake in the form of a dashing young nobleman with his man servant in tow. The visitor claimed to be Zhuang's dedicated student, and as Zhuang's house was in the middle of nowhere, he was invited to put up at the house.*
>
> *Zhuang's widow was so taken by this handsome and well-bred stranger that within a matter of weeks, and even before the casket was buried (they were obviously waiting for a good date), she took the initiative to propose marriage. To cut a long story short, the casket containing Zhuang's body was relegated to a storeroom, and a simple wedding ceremony was conducted.*
>
> *Just as the couple was about to turn in for the night, the groom suddenly collapsed in an epileptic fit. His man servant told the frantic bride this happened before, and the cure was to administer a potion made from human cranial fluid. Whereas it was possible to obtain such a prescription in the city by executing a convicted criminal, this was obviously not possible in the circumstances.*
>
> *But there was a dead body available, the bride thought. After ascertaining that the cranial fluid of a relatively new corpse would do the trick, she took an axe, went to the storeroom, and hacked open the casket, whereupon her erstwhile husband calmly sat up, quite alive.*

Ode to Mysticism

Chapter 1.3: "Control" (Clash) Interactions

> *When the plot was revealed, the woman was so ashamed she hanged herself. Zhuang laid her body in the casket originally meant for him, sat by its side, and in a melancholic mood, composed poetry drumming on an earthenware basin to keep the beat. That done, he smashed the basin, set fire to the place, casket, house and all; and walked away to start a new life. He did not marry again.*
>
> *Somehow this melodramatic tale survived the centuries and became known as the story of "Zhuang Sheng drumming on a basin" (莊生鼓盆).*
>
> *On reflection, shouldn't the guy be arrested and charged for conspiracy to murder, with arson thrown in for good measure? But in those days, a wife's fidelity vows were expected to survive death – his death of course. Husbands weren't required to take such vows. Whoever said man and woman were created equal?*

4-6 represents a relationship between an elderly man (Star-6, *yang* Metal) and a much younger woman (Star-4, *yin* Wood) - a delicate situation to say the least. The woman suffers at the hands of the man. Now a Wood-Metal conflict is hardly beneficial, but for it to be dire enough to kill off one's wife is going a bit far, don't you think? ☹

[In "Secrets of *xuan kong*" Line SX54, it is mentioned that 4-6, if corroborated by a waterway looping round from *xun* to *qian*, points to suicide by hanging.]

Fig-110 shows a Period-7 property Sitting *xun* Facing *qian*. There is a 4-6 conjunction at *zhen*. Now if the door or bedroom is located at *zhen*, it points to a strained relationship between husband and wife. Having Water at *zhen* palace should mitigate the problem, as Water mediates between Metal and Wood.

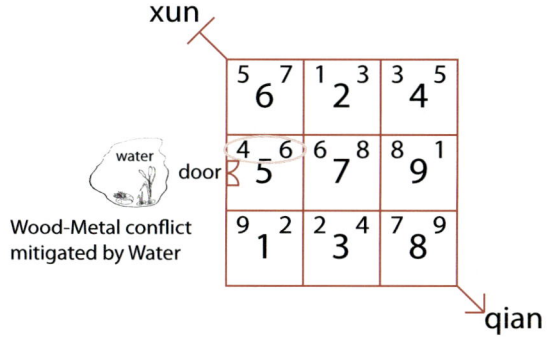

Fig-110: 4-6 conjunction

Chapter 1.3: "Control" (Clash) Interactions

> **OM31:** 坎流坤位，賈臣常遭賤婦之羞。
>
> When water from *kan* (Star-1) flows into *kun* (Star-2), the humiliation of Jia Chen by his despicable wife will be reenacted. [Idiom describing a bullying wife, see box]

The line describes a 1-2 conjunction, i.e. *yang* Water controlled by *yin* Earth.

The background story is narrated below.

> *The story of Jia Chen's humiliation:*
>
> *The character in this story was a scholar by the name of Zhu Jia Chen (朱買臣), circa 110 BCE. Zhu was destitute and etched out a meagre living cutting firewood. Like other scholars of his time, his burning ambition was to pass the public exams and become a government official.*
>
> *Zhu had a lazy good-for-nothing wife who resented the poverty in which they lived. Not only was she unsupportive of his efforts, she nagged him day and night using disdainful and abusive language. Being of a gentle disposition, Zhu merely cajoled her to wait for the day he realized his ambition.*
>
> *But the woman's displeasure only worsened. She demanded for a divorce so that she could go her own way. Zhu said "To write a divorce paper is easy, but like water thrown out, to retrieve it is not that simple." His wife was adamant, threatening suicide if he refused. So Zhu reluctantly wrote the paper, and she left.*
>
> *Several years later, Zhu managed to pass the exams at national level. He was appointed an official, and as was customary, his triumphant return to his village on horseback was a grand event. His ex-wife heard the news and came forward seeking forgiveness and pleading with him to take her back.*
>
> *Zhu coolly took a basin of water, splashed it on the ground, and told the woman, "Now you try to put the water back into the basin."*
>
> *This story became known as "Jia Chen parting with his wife" (賈臣別妻), or "Splashing water before the horse" (馬前潑水).*

46 Ode to Mysticism

Chapter 1.3: "Control" (Clash) Interactions

When the Stars are untimely and/or aggravated by external landforms, a 1-2 conjunction points to a man being bullied by his wife.

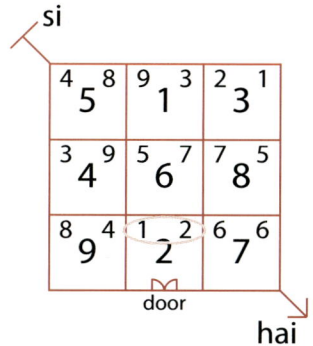

Fig-111: 1-2 conjunction

Take the case of Fig-111, a Period-6 property Sitting *si* Facing *hai*. If the door is opened at *kan* palace where the conjunction 1-2 resides, we can predict that the woman "wears the pants" in the household.

PART-1
"Ode to Mysticism (玄機賦)"
the xuan kong Interpretation

Chapter 1.4

Health Issues

Chapter 1.4
Health Issues

> **OM32:** 艮非宜也，筋傷股折。
>
> If *gen* (Star-8) is unwell, tendons will be hurt and the thighbone fractures.

gen (Star-8) is associated with the backbone and limbs.

"Unwell" means the Star is untimely and afflicted by negative landforms.

When Star-8 is afflicted, the problems could include: fractured limbs; locomotive disorder; rheumatoid arthritis; neurological disorders; etc.

[Similar to Secrets of *xuan kong* Line SX63]

Chapter 1.4: Health Issues

OM33: 兌不利歟，唇亡齒寒。

What if *dui* (Star-7) is disadvantaged? The demise of the lips will expose the teeth to bitter cold. [Idiom, see sidebar]

dui (Star-7) relates to the mouth. An untimely Star-7 aggravated by negative landforms could indicate a cleft lip or other mouth related problems.

Other problems associated with Star-7 include: dental complaints; cough; throat infections; speech impediments; lung infections; menstrual issues; sexually transmitted diseases; wounded by a knife; etc.

The phrase "demise of the lips exposing the teeth to bitter cold (唇亡齒寒)" is in fact a well known idiom explained in the sidebar, but by a twist of poetic licence, the idiomatic meaning is abandoned in this instance in favour of the mundane interpretation of a cleft lip.

As I mentioned in the Introduction, the author Wu Jing Luan (吳景鸞) had a streak of the maverick in him. Looks like he enjoyed his little mind games with his readers.

[Similar to Secrets of *xuan kong* Line SX62]

> "Demise of the lips exposing the teeth to bitter cold":
>
> This proverb originated from the Spring & Autumn Period of Chinese history (770~476 BCE). The Duchy of Jin (晉), one of the larger states, wanted to attack a small neighbour called the Duchy of Guo (虢). To get to Guo, Jin's army had to pass through another small territory called the Duchy of Lu (虞).
>
> So the Duke of Jin asked for the Duke of Lu's cooperation and offered him gifts of precious jade and sleek horses. One of Lu's advisers by the name of Gong Zhi Qi (宮之奇) promptly cautioned the Duke, saying that Lu and Guo were two small states that depended on each other like the lips and the teeth. If the lips ceased to exist, the teeth could not survive the cold.
>
> But the Duke of Lu was tempted and agreed to help Jin against Guo. In due course Jin conquered Guo, and on the return journey swallowed up Lu as well. The jade and horses went back to Jin.
>
> The proverb is used to describe two interdependent parties that will survive or perish together.

Ode to Mysticism

Chapter 1.4: Health Issues

> **OM34:** 坎宮缺陷而墮胎；離位巉巖而損目。
>
> A missing or sunken *kan* palace (Star-1) will lead to miscarriage. Jagged rocks at *li* location (Star-9) will impair one's sight.

kan (Star-1) relates to the following body parts and systems: ears; urinary system; reproductive organs; arteries; intelligence; etc.

When the text says "missing or sunken", it implies a serious defect with *kan* palace or Star-1, and not necessarily a missing palace or deep ravine at *kan*, although such properties tend to be more susceptible.

If Star-1 is untimely and there are negative landforms outside, irrespective of the palace at which Star-1 resides, then the same prediction applies.

The line mentions miscarriage, but that is only by way of example.

[Similar to Secrets of *xuan kong* Line SX60]

li (Star-9) relates to the eyes and the heart.

If there are unsightly rock faces outside *li* palace, or the palace at which Star-9 resides, and Star-9 is untimely, then the residents are susceptible to eyes and heart ailments.

Sharp rocky outcrops, typically uneven rock faces after quarrying operations or exposed rocky cliffs thanks to irresponsible developers, are particularly injurious to health. If the Stars at the afflicted palace are also detrimental, then we can predict health issues with confidence.

[Similar to Secrets of *xuan kong* Line SX61]

Ode to Mysticism

PART-1
"Ode to Mysticism (玄機賦)"
the xuan kong Interpretation

Chapter 1.5
Glad Tidings

Chapter 1.5
Glad Tidings

> **OM35:** 輔臨丁丙，位列朝班。
>
> When "Left Assistant" (Star-8) approaches *bing* and *ding* (Star-9), one will have a place in the Emperor's morning audience.

The word "Assist (輔)" is open to different interpretations. The popular interpretation is that it refers to the "Left Assistant Star (左輔星)" of the North Dipper Asterism, which is a synonym of Star-8.

"*bing* and *ding*" clearly refers to Star-9.

If that interpretation is adopted, then Line OM35 describes an 8-9 conjunction, i.e. a Fire growing Earth interaction.

"Emperor's morning audience" implies high office. [See sidebar]

For this to happen, both Stars-8 & 9 must be timely. Needless to say, the Stars must also be supported by favourable landforms.

What if the Stars are untimely and/or afflicted by negative landforms? Then the prediction will be quite different. The Earth of Star-8 will be scorched by the Fire of Star-9. The affected individual can forget about high office. He will even have difficulty passing his exams.

[Secrets of *xuan kong* Line SX20 says 8-9 produces idiots]

> *Traditionally, the Emperor (only the hardworking ones of course) used to hold an audience in the morning, at which senior ministers and generals would stand in line, ready to discuss matters of state.*
>
> *Obviously, to be included in this high level assembly, one would need to be a Cabinet minister or an armed forces chief.*

Fig-112 shows a Period-8 property Sitting *xun* Facing *qian*. The chart is "Prosperous Sitting Prosperous Facing (旺山旺向)", which has good potential, provided of course the external landforms are supportive. Note that there is an 8-9 conjunction between the Facing Star and the Period Star at *qian* palace. The career prospects of the male head of household are excellent, provided he can avoid the "Fire Burning Heaven's Gate" problem (6-9 at *qian*). [Shouldn't be a problem if there are no negative forms at *qian*, and the stove is not placed there.] In the year when Annual

Chapter 1.5: Glad Tidings

Star-8 flies into the centre (as for example 2010 *geng yin*) thus delivering Star-9 to *qian*, his chances of promotion with good emoluments will be redoubled.

Another interpretation says the word "Assist (輔)" refers to the "Heavenly Assistant Star (天輔星)", which is an alias of the "Literary Arts Star (文曲星)" (Star-4, Wood).

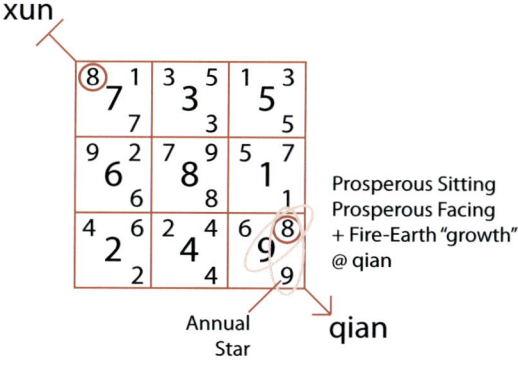

Fig-112: 8-9 conjunction

If this interpretation is adopted, Line OM35 describes a Wood-Fire "growth" interaction. Wood growing Fire stands for brilliance, meaning superior intelligence. Well, one certainly needs to be intelligent to make it to the position of cabinet minister [although sometimes I wonder].

One problem is Stars-4 & 9 cannot be timely at the same time. Wood (Star-4) would definitely need to be timely in order to grow Fire (Star-9). Even if Star-9 is untimely, it can be bolstered up by its location at a Wood or Fire palace, and/or the presence of other Wood or Fire Stars. Needless to say, landform support is a prerequisite.

There is a 3rd interpretation, the landform version. The word "Assist (輔)" now refers to a "Left Assistant Embrace (左輔砂)", which is of Wood element, and represents capable supporters. Line OM35 says that if such a mound is found at the *bing* and *ding* sectors of the *luo pan*, measured from the subject property of course, then the indications are that the household will produce capable persons who will rise to ministerial (or CEO of large corporations) status.

Why *bing* and *ding* sectors? That's because at *bing* there is the "Heavenly Noble Star (天貴星)", and at *ding* there is the "Southern Dipper Star (南極星)". Both these Stars in the Southern skies are top grade beneficial Stars. In the study of the Heavenly Stars, they are 2 members of the group called the "3 Auspicious 6 Elegance (三吉六秀)".

In fact there is a common thread all the way from Line OM35 to Line OM38, where the lines can be explained in terms of landforms.

Ode to Mysticism

Chapter 1.5: Glad Tidings

OM36: 巨入坤艮，田連阡陌。

When "Huge Door" (Star-2) enters (meets with) *kun* (Star-2) and *gen* (Star-8), farmlands will number in the hundreds and thousands.

"Huge Door" = Star-2; *kun* = Star-2; *gen* = Star-8.

In the Flying Stars interpretation, the line describes a 2-2 or 2-8 conjunction.

In both cases, it is Earth meeting Earth, making more Earth. Star-2 represents farmlands and property wealth – hence the prognosis of wealth through vast land holdings.

Fig-113 shows a Period-8 property Sitting *shen* Facing *yin*. There are 2-8 conjunctions at *kun*, *gen* and the central palace. If there is water outside *kun*, and there is a *qi* mouth (door) at *kun*, we can predict that the residents will do well in property businesses. This is in spite of the fact that the chart is "Up Mountain Down Water".

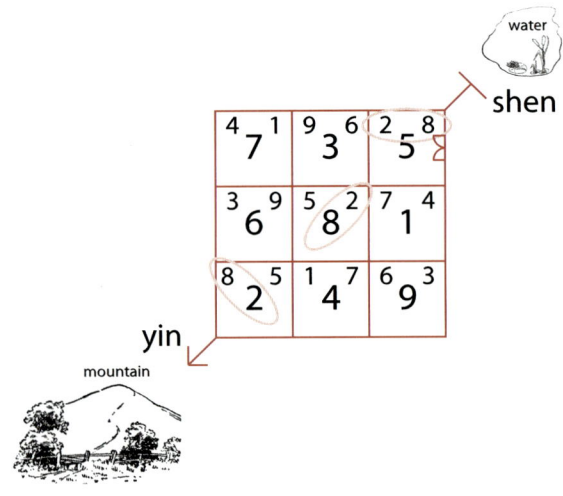

Fig-113: 2-8 conjunction

This example demonstrates that "Up Mountain Down Water" charts are not necessarily bad. In this case, if the terrain is higher at the front (Northeast) and lower at the back (Southwest), then the chart is supported, and if the Stars are used properly the outcome can be very positive indeed.

For a prediction of wealth to hold true, the Stars (or at least one of them) must be timely and the external landforms amply supportive. Otherwise, 2-8 indicates spirituality more than wealth.

["Secrets of *xuan kong*" Line SX80 says 2-8 produces monks and nuns.]

In the landforms version, "Huge Door" is a large rectangular shaped mountain with a flat top. It is of Earth element, and stands for wealth.

If such a mountain is seen at *kun* or *gen* (in each case the 15° sector, not the whole palace), then it is a sure sign of landed property wealth.

Why *kun* or *gen*? At *gen* in the Northeastern skies, there is the "Heavenly City Asterism (天市垣)", another member of the "3 Auspicious 6 Elegance (三吉六秀)" group. This asterism is especially good for commerce. [Chinese astrology does not differentiate between asterisms, stars and planets. They are all called "Stars".]

kun is "Mother Earth (地母)". Although there are no beneficial Heavenly Stars of comparable standing at that sector of the Southwestern skies, it benefits from a reflection of the "Heavenly City Asterism" diametrically opposite. Moreover *kun* represents productive land that has an enormous capacity to absorb and produce – hence the prognosis of "hundreds and thousands of farmlands".

Chapter 1.5: Glad Tidings

> **OM37:** 名揚科第，貪狼星在巽宮。
>
> When "Greedy Wolf" (Star-1) is located at *xun* palace (Star-4), one's reputation will spread through the exams.

This line describes a 1-4 Star conjunction. The same topic is covered in Line OM26 earlier. There is little need to elaborate further.

In the landforms version, "Greedy Wolf" is typically a pyramid shaped mountain with a blunted top. [This is typical only. "Greedy Wolf" mountains come in a wide range of shapes and sizes.] It is of the Wood element, and stands for nobility, high status, helpful persons, etc.

At the *xun* (15°) sector of the Southeastern skies, there is the "Greater Covert Asterism (太微垣)", a very noble Star that represents high office. In addition to being a member of the "3 Auspicious 6 Elegance (三吉六秀)" group, it is also one of the "Heavenly Stars 4 Nobles (天星四貴)".

Hence if a "Greedy Wolf" mountain is seen outside *xun* palace, it is as if the "Greater Covert Asterism" has landed, bringing with it the status and spoils of high office.

Chapter 1.5: Glad Tidings

> **OM38:** 職掌兵權，武曲峰當庚兌。
>
> When a "Military Arts" mountain (Star-6) meets with *geng* and *dui* (Star-7), military power will be to hand.

The line describes a 6-7 Star conjunction.

It says that a 6-7 conjunction signifies military power in one's hands. This is only the case if the Stars are timely and the external landforms are supportive. Failing that, a 6-7 conjunction is called "Cross Swords Killing (交劍殺)". It denotes conflict, robbery and the spilling of blood. [see Line OM19]

In the landforms version, "Military Arts" is a low bun shaped mountain. It signals military power, and in modern society, executive authority and responsibility.

At the *geng* sector of the Western skies, there is the "Military Baron (武爵)" Star; and at *dui* (in the present context read as *you*) there is the "Lesser Covert Asterism (少微垣)", another of the "3 Auspicious 6 Elegance (三吉六秀)" and "Heavenly Stars 4 Nobles (天星四貴)".

If a "Military Arts" mountain is seen outside *geng* or *you*, the Star's influence is greatly amplified by the landform.

Ode to Mysticism

PART-1
"Ode to Mysticism (玄機賦)"
the xuan kong Interpretation

Chapter 1.6

And So On...

Chapter 1.6
And So On...

OM39: 乾首坤腹，八卦推詳。

qian represents the head and *kun* the belly. Such associations may be derived from the 8 Trigrams.

OM40: 癸足丁心，十干類取。

gui represents the feet and *ding* the heart. Such associations may be obtained from the 10 stems.

These 2 lines point out that the human body parts are associated with certain Trigrams and Heavenly Stems (and by implication also Earthly Branches), and ailments of these body parts are often reflected in defects of these Metaphysical entities, such as an elemental clash or the presence of negative landforms.

Modern medicine would of course dispute, even ridicule, such a connection. Yet alternative medicine is slowly gaining ground in modern society, and if there is a chance for an ailment to be alleviated by fixing certain Metaphysical defects, what is the harm in that?

The table below lists the body parts associated with each Trigram, Heavenly Stem and Earthly Branch:

qian	乾	head; brains; lungs
dui	兌	mouth; lips; teeth; lungs
li	離	eyes; heart
zhen	震	legs; gall bladder
xun	巽	thighs; pelvis; liver
kan	坎	ears; kidneys; uterus
gen	艮	hands; digits; spinal column; nose
kun	坤	abdomen; stomach; skin

Chapter 1.6: And So On...

jia	甲	head
yi	乙	neck
bing	丙	shoulders
ding	丁	heart
wu	戊	flank
ji	己	spleen
geng	庚	navel
xin	辛	thighs
ren	壬	shins
gui	癸	feet

zi	子	genitals
chou	丑	spleen; liver
yin	寅	thighs; upper arms
mao	卯	eyes; hands
chen	辰	back; chest
si	巳	face; teeth
wu	午	heart; abdomen
wei	未	spleen; flank
shen	申	bronchia
you	酉	back; lungs
xu	戌	head; neck
hai	亥	liver; kidneys

Chapter 1.6: And So On...

> **OM41:** 木入坎宮，鳳池身貴。
>
> Wood (Star-4 rather than Star-3) entering *kan* palace (Star-1) provides one with high enough status to be admitted to the "Phoenix Pool".

This line once again describes a 1-4 conjunction. See Lines OM26 and OM37.

Historically, "Phoenix Pool" was a recreational place frequented by the high and mighty, much like certain exclusive social clubs today.

It should be 1-4 and not 1-3 because 1-4 satisfies *yin-yang* pairing, whereas 1-3 does not.

Line OM25 already said 1-3 makes fickle acquaintances.

Chapter 1.6: And So On...

OM42: 金居艮位，烏府求名。

Metal (Star-7 rather than Star-6) occupying *gen* location (Star-8) represents a person seeking a position at the "House of Ravens".

The conjunction 7-8 also indicates success. It is an Earth-Metal "growth" interaction that also satisfies *yin-yang* pairing.

Traditionally, success was measured in terms of one's position in the civil or military service. "House of Ravens" is a metaphor for high office. [See sidebar]

> *It was said that during the Han Dynasty, a flock of ravens roosted on a cypress tree at the building housing the Emperor's private secretariat. Henceforth the offices of the Emperor's trusted aides were given the moniker "House of Ravens".*

Like 1-4, 7-8 provides a means of entry into the corridors of power, but the routes differ. Whereas 1-4 represents admission through the traditional exams and working one's way diligently to the top, 7-8 represents what is euphemistically called "alternative road to success (異路功名)".

It used to be a polite way of implying that a person has bought himself a coveted position, but to be more charitable, let's say if a person is honoured publicly for his notable achievements in business, academia, the arts, sports, community service, etc., that would also count as an "alternative road to success" in modern times.

It is evident the line refers more to 7-8 than 6-8, as Line OM18 already said that 6-8, being a *yang-yang* relationship, is less desirable.

7-8 is also discussed in Line OM17.

Chapter 1.6: And So On...

> **OM43:** 金取土培，火宜木相。
>
> Metal seeks the nourishment of Earth, just as Fire desires the companionship of Wood.

This line appears to be a very general statement that reaffirms the Earth-Metal and Wood-Fire "growth" relationships.

As these relationships have already been discussed at length elsewhere in the poem, the raison d'être of this line is unclear.

The contemporary writer Bai He Ming (白鶴鳴) suggested that Metal-Earth here refers to 6-8, and Wood-Fire refers to 4-9. Both are uni-polar "growth" interactions, quite useless for procreation [see Line OM18], but highly beneficial for other purposes.

Both represent success in one's endeavours, but there is a marked difference: 6-8 being *yang* represents the more aggressive type of success such as a high ranking military officer or a champion in sports; whereas 4-9 being *yin* represents the more reserved type of success such as wide acclaim as an academician, writer, artist, and so on. In other words, it's "the power of the sword" compared with "the power of the pen".

This is the last line of the poem "Ode to Mysticism (玄機賦)", but it doesn't look like a closing line at all. It is most unusual for a classical treatise to end so abruptly. Possibly parts of the poem were lost through the ages, or the author, Wu Jing Luan (吳景鸞), did not complete the task for one reason or another.

The similarity of this poem to the author's other major *xuan kong* treatise, "Secrets of *xuan kong* (玄空秘旨)", also poses the question: why 2 poems so closely related? It doesn't look as if one is an addendum or a clarification of the other. Did Master Wu have something else in mind?

It is possible to interpret the poem "Ode to Mysticism (玄機賦)" in the language of 8-Mansions (八宅) *fengshui*. Now the *xuan kong* and 8-Mansions schools were historically bitter rivals. Was Master Wu such a maverick to have preached 8-Mansions in the guise of a *xuan kong* poem? It is an interesting poser.

In Part-2, we shall re-examine the poem from the 8-Mansions perspective.

PART-2
"Ode to Mysticism (玄機賦)"
The 8-Mansions Interpretation

PART-2
"Ode to Mysticism (玄機賦)"
The 8-Mansions Interpretation

Chapter 2.1

Stars & Palaces

Chapter 2.1
Stars & Palaces

8M01: 大哉！居乎成敗所係；危哉！葬也興廢攸關。

Grossly so! Success or failure is dependent on the house. Gravely so! Ascendance or futility is determined by burial.

In this first line, the interpretation is the same as in Part-1.

The *fengshui* of a house, called "*yang* dwelling (陽宅)", affects the residents' success or failure in life, whereas the burial ground, called "*yin* dwelling (陰宅)", affects the fate of future generations.

Chapter 2.1
Stars & Palaces

> **8M02:** 氣口司一宅之樞，龍穴樂三吉之輔。
>
> The *qi* mouth serves as the pivot of the house. The meridian spot desires the support of the 3 Auspicious.

The main door of a house is its primary "*qi* mouth (氣口)". As the residents move through this door, they carry the *qi* of the environment into the house. In 8-Mansions, as in other *fengshui* disciplines, the main door constitutes one of 3 key features of a house, the other 2 being the bed and the stove.

The back door, other secondary doors and even large windows are also *qi* mouths of sorts, but they are of less importance than the main door.

"meridian spot", in this context, refers to a tomb.

"3 Auspicious" refers to the 3 major auspicious "Wandering Stars (遊星)" under the 8-Mansions system, these being: "*sheng qi* (生氣)"; "*tian yi* (天醫)"; and "*yan nian* (延年)".

As the main door of a house is so important, it should be located at one of these 3 auspicious locations. That's the easy part. But what is meant by a tomb needing the support of these 3 Stars?

8-Mansions is by and large a "*yang* dwelling" technique. To apply the technique to a tomb is unusual. How do we divide a tomb into 8 palaces? We can only surmise that in Master Wu's days, 8-Mansions was indeed used for "*yin* dwellings".

For the line to make sense, we need to look at the surroundings of the tomb. The Sitting of the tomb is its reference Trigram, or "*fu wei* (伏位)". If there are landforms like charismatic mountains, elegant structures, or access road at the directions corresponding to the "*sheng qi* (生氣)", "*tian yi* (天醫)" or "*yan nian* (延年)" of the reference Trigram, then the tomb is said to have the support of these auspicious Stars.

Now it is widely known there are altogether 4 auspicious "Wandering Stars" in the 8-Mansions system: "*sheng qi* (生氣)", "*tian yi* (天醫)", "*yan nian* (延年)" and "*fu wei* (伏位)'. Why is "*fu wei*" left out?

Chapter 2.1: Stars & Palaces

It is because *"fu wei"* is located at the reference Trigram of the property. It is the identity of the property. The other 3 auspicious Stars are defined with reference to *"fu wei"*.

In fact, landforms outside *"fu wei"* at the back of the property are very important. They are usually part of the "Incoming Dragon (入首龍)" that determines the overall quality of the land. But we are digressing into landform *fengshui*. Let's get back to 8-Mansions.

This book does not set out to teach 8-Mansions. It is assumed readers are already familiar with the system's fundamentals, but as "Wandering Stars" constitute the backbone of the 8-Mansions system, I thought a brief revision in the form of Appendix-1 could be useful.

Chapter 2.1: Stars & Palaces

> **8M03:** 陰陽雖云四路，宗支只有兩家。
>
> Although it is said there are 4 roads of *yin-yang*, at the source there are only 2 families.

"4 roads of *yin-yang*" refers to the 4 natural *yin-yang* pairs within the 8 Trigrams, these being:

qian (*yang*) pairs with *kun* (*yin*);
zhen (*yang*) pairs with *xun* (*yin*);
kan (*yang*) pairs with *li* (*yin*);
gen (*yang*) pairs with *dui* (*yin*).

Line 8M03 says even though there are 4 such pairs, they ultimately fall into 2 families, these being:

"East Group" comprising of *zhen*, *xun*, *kan* and *li*;
"West Group" comprising of *qian*, *kun*, *gen*, and *dui*.

Chapter 2.1: Stars & Palaces

> **8M04:** 數列五行，體用恩仇始見。
>
> There are 5 Metaphysical elements. Their "Body" and "Application" will reveal the benefactor and enemy.

The 5 Metaphysical elements are of course Wood, Fire, Earth, Metal and Water.

"Body (體) and Application (用)" is a difficult concept. Almost every *fengshui* classic mentions "Body" and "Application", but none has bothered to provide a comprehensive definition thereof. Perhaps there isn't one. The term is fluidic enough to fit into different shapes in different contexts.

In the present context, "Body" refers to the palace itself, and "Application" refers to the "Wandering Star" that resides at the said palace in a given property. To be precise, it is their respective elements that count.

The term "benefactor and enemy" is simply another way of saying "auspicious and inauspicious" or "beneficial and detrimental".

Line 8M04 implies that whether a palace is beneficial or otherwise for a particular purpose is determined by the palace element and the Star element. This statement hints at the principle of "Star-Palace Interaction (星宮生剋)", which plays an important role in advanced 8-Mansions.

However, I consider it premature to introduce this principle at this early stage. We shall revisit the topic shortly. For the time being, it is sufficient to think of the need to match the elements of the usable palaces (where the 3 key features are located) with the reference (Sitting) palace in any one group, i.e. Water/Wood/Fire in one group, Earth/Metal in the other.

To elaborate: in a East Group house, the usable palaces are Water *kan* (Water), *zhen* and *xun* (Wood), *li* (Fire); whereas in a West Group house, the usable palaces are *gen* and *kun* (Earth), *qian* and *dui* (Metal).

Chapter 2.1: Stars & Palaces

> **8M05:** 星分九曜，吉凶悔吝斯彰。
>
> There are 9 different Stars. Their beneficial or detrimental status will make clear whether the outcome is regretful or precious.

In 8-Mansions, there are only 8 "Wandering Stars (遊星)", which are:

➢ the 4 beneficial Stars - "*sheng qi* (生氣)", "*tian yi* (天醫)", "*yan nian* (延年)", "*fu wei* (伏位)"; and

➢ the 4 harmful Stars - "*huo hai* (禍害)", "*liu sha* (六殺)", "*wu gui* (五鬼)", "*jue ming* (絕命)".

Yet the line says there are 9 different Stars. How so?

The "Wandering Stars" of 8-Mansions are linked to the "North Dipper Asterism (北斗星)", a collection of physical stars in the Northern skies, in the following way:

Wandering Stars	North Dipper Stars		
	Chinese Name	Greek Name	Modern Ref.
sheng qi (生氣)	Greedy Wolf (貪狼)	Dubhe	αUMa
tian yi (天醫)	Huge Door (巨門)	Merak	βUMa
huo hai (禍害)	Rewards (祿存)	Phecda	γUMa
liu sha (六殺)	Literary Arts (文曲)	Megrez	δUMa
wu gui (五鬼)	Chastity (廉貞)	Alioth	εUMa
yan nian (延年)	Military Arts (武曲)	Mizar	ζUMa
jue ming (絕命)	Broken Soldier (破軍)	Alkaid	ηUMa
fu wei (伏位)	Left Assistant (左輔) & Right Assistant (右弼)	Alcor (none)	80UMa M101

According to the Chinese astronomers, the "North Dipper" has 9 Stars. In order to fit the 8 "Wandering Stars" into the 9 Stars of the "North Dipper", 8-Mansions assigned both the "Left Assistant" and "Right Assistant" to "*fu wei*".

Chapter 2.1: Stars & Palaces

Each of the "Wandering Stars" is further assigned certain attributes with which all students of 8-Mansions should be familiar.

Further information on the "North Dipper" Stars and the "Wandering Star" attributes are provided in Appendix-1.

Line 8M05 says that the attributes of the "Wandering Stars" is an important factor in determining the suitability of a location for an intended purpose.

For example, *"sheng qi"* would be eminently suitable for locating a door, especially for a business premise, but because of its hyper-active character, *"sheng qi"* would not make a good choice for a bedroom.

Reading Lines 8M04 and 8M05 together (the lines are 2 parts a couplet), it is abundantly clear that the correct use of the palaces according to their East/West grouping, as well as the intrinsic attributes of the "Wandering Star", are critical in deciding whether a location is suitable for the purpose intended.

Chapter 2.1: Stars & Palaces

> **8M06:** 宅神不可損傷，用神最宜健旺。
>
> The "House God" should not be hurt. It is best for the "Useful Gods" to be healthy and prosperous.

"House God" refers to the reference Trigram of the house, i.e. the Sitting of the house. For example, the Trigram of a South Sitting house would be *li*.

The Sitting palace of the house should be wholesome, i.e. it should not be missing, incomplete or threatened by any form of *sha qi* (煞氣). For example, a U-shaped floor plan with the concave part at the back would be regarded as a missing Sitting palace. External *sha qi* could come in the form of rocky outcrops, "Reverse Bow (反弓)" river/road, T-junction, electric pylon, "Sky Crack Killing (天斬煞)", "Flying Blade Killing (飛刃煞)", etc. Any of these will destabilize the *qi* of the house.

"Useful Gods" refers to the palaces at which the 3 key features, door bed and stove, are located. It is also important for these palaces to be wholesome and free of *sha qi*.

In addition, the door and bed should be located at a positive "Wandering Star", i.e. "*sheng qi*", "*tian yi*", "*yan nian*" or "*fu wei*". Of that there is no dispute. As to the location of the stove, there is an unresolved dispute amongst 8-Mansions scholars.

The influential 8-Mansions text "8-Mansions Bright Mirror (八宅明鏡)" and its sister text "Golden Light Star Arrival Classic (金光斗臨經)" advocated that the stove should be located at a negative "Wandering Star" (i.e. "*huo hai*", "*liu sha*", "*wu gui*" or "*jue ming*"), so that the smoke, soot, and other nasties will suppress the negative Star [talking about "sh***ing" on the enemy... ☺]. But whither the smoke and soot in our modern gas or electric stove?

"Bright Mirror" and "Golden Light" are relatively late writings (Qing Dynasty, 18th Century). If one were to research into earlier 8-Mansions texts (17th Century and earlier), one would find that they recommended the stove to be located at a positive Star instead. Their argument was straightforward: as the stove governed food intake and hence the health of the household, it should be located at a positive Star to absorb the Star's positive attributes.

This is not the right platform to debate this point. I only mentioned it because the "Ode to Mysticism" was written in the Song Dynasty, a good 700 years before "Bright Mirror" and "Golden Light". At the time of the "Ode", it was likely 8-Mansions treated the stove the same way as the door and bed.

Chapter 2.1: Stars & Palaces

> **8M07:** 值難不傷，蓋因難歸閒地。
>
> If the presence of a disastrous entity does not inflict damage, it is because the disastrous entity resides at a passive location.

"Disastrous entity" refers to a negative "Wandering Star": "*huo hai* (禍害)", "*liu sha* (六殺)", "*wu gui* (五鬼)" or "*jue ming* (絕命)".

The line says if an important feature, say the door, is located at a negative Star but nothing untoward happens, it is because the negative Star is located at a palace where it is comparatively harmless.

Where would that be?

The answer lies in a key 8-Mansions principle called "Star-Palace Interaction (星宮生剋)". We can devote a whole chapter to the discussion of this vital principle, but I would leave the details to dedicated 8-Mansions papers or study programs.

For our present purpose, we will summarize by saying that in 8-Mansions, the suitability and efficacy of a location for a particular purpose is evaluated based on 2 Metaphysical entities at that location: one is the Trigram of the location (*qian* at NW; *kun* at SW; etc.); the other is the "Wandering Star" ("*sheng qi*", "*tian yi*", etc.) that lands at the said location in a given property.

The Trigram and the "Wandering Star" each has its own element. The interaction between these 2 elements is an important factor in determining how good a location is for the intended purpose. A "growth" and "co-prosperous" interaction is positive; "control" is negative.

[The weakening cycle is ignored. For example, Wood palace with Fire Star is not read as Wood being depleted by Fire and therefore negative. The emphasis is on "mutual growth (相生)", i.e. as long as one element grows the other, the interaction is deemed positive.

Likewise, the difference between "control-in" and "control-out" is disregarded. A "control" interaction, either way, is deemed negative.

An in-depth discussion of "Star-Palace Interaction" is provided in Appendix-2. The discussion goes much beyond our present deliberations, but the more inquisitive readers may find it interesting.]

Take the case of a *li* house which has its "*sheng qi*" at *zhen* palace. Now "*sheng qi*" is of Wood element; the Trigram *zhen* is also Wood. Hence it is a Wood Star at a Wood palace, which makes the palace very vibrant. A door located at *zhen* would be highly beneficial.

On the other hand, the same house has its *"tian yi"* at *xun*. *"tian yi"* is Earth, but *xun* is Wood. A door at *xun* would be compromised by the Wood-Earth conflict.

Conversely, in a South seated *li* house, *"jue ming"* lands at *qian* palace. Now *"jue ming"* is a Metal Star and *qian* is also Metal. *"jue ming"* therefore feels at ease and is disinclined to be aggressive. Another way of saying this is that *"jue ming"* resides at a passive location.

On the other hand, in the same house, *"wu gui"* lands at *dui* palace. *"wu gui"* is Fire but *dui* is Metal. Hence there is a Fire-Metal clash at *dui*. *"wu gui"* is in unfriendly territory and can be expected to react aggressively.

Chapter 2.1: Stars & Palaces

> **8M08:** 逢恩不發，祇緣恩落仇宮。
>
> If one does not profit from meeting a benefactor, it is only because the benefactor has fallen into an enemy palace.

"benefactor" refers to a positive "Wandering Star": "*sheng qi* (生氣)", "*tian yi* (天醫)", "*yan nian* (延年)" or "*fu wei* (伏位)".

The line says that if an important feature, like the door, is located at one of these positive Stars but good fortune eludes the household, it is because the positive Star is located at an unfriendly palace.

Take the case of a West seated *dui* house. Its "*sheng qi*" is located at *qian*. Now, "*sheng qi*" is Wood whereas *qian* is Metal. If the house has its main door at *qian*, the benefits of a "*sheng qi*" door may not be forthcoming as there is a Metal-Wood conflict at that palace.

It is worth noting that the different elemental conflicts have different degrees of severity and different outcomes:

- Metal-Wood conflict is the most damaging - the Wood is cut and the Metal blunted;

- Fire-Metal conflict tends to be sudden and explosive, but the end result may turn positive;

- Water-Fire conflict transforms both elements, meaning that the outcome is often a totally new situation;

- Earth-Water conflict results in the Water being controlled and redirected, which is not necessarily a bad thing, but the Earth is eroded and contaminated;

- Wood-Earth conflict is the least antagonistic. Although the 2 elements are nominally in conflict, Wood and Earth are also mutually dependent: Wood ventilates Earth making it productive; Earth in turn provides support to the growing Wood.

Chapter 2.1: Stars & Palaces

> **8M09:** 一貴當權，諸凶懾服。
>
> One beneficial Star in power will cause multiple harmful entities to submit in fear.

This line describes the main door, it being the most critical of the 3 key features of a house (door, bed, stove).

If the "Wandering Star" at the door is "*sheng qi*", "*tian yi*" or "*yan nian*" ("*fu wei*" is deemed too passive for use at the main door), and the element of the palace supports the Star, then the Star is said to be "in power". This is provided there is no *sha qi* outside to defeat the setup.

With such a powerful door, the negative Stars, namely "*huo hai*", "*liu sha*", "*wu gui*" and "*jue ming*", at the house will be subdued and rendered harmless.

Chapter 2.1: Stars & Palaces

> **8M10:** 眾凶剋主，獨力難支。
>
> If multiple harmful Stars control the principal, it will be difficult for a lone force to withstand the pressure.

"principal" here refers to the Trigram of the house, at which the Star "*fu wei*" resides.

If the 3 key features of the house are located at the negative Stars, or at positive Stars rendered ineffective by the "Star-Palace Interaction" principle, or the palace is hurt by external *sha qi*, then "*fu wei*" cannot be relied upon to fend off the ill effects.

PART-2
"Ode to Mysticism (玄機賦)"
The 8-Mansions Interpretation

Chapter 2.2

East Group West Group

Chapter 2.2
East Group West Group

8M11: 火炎土燥，南離何益乎艮坤。

A hot fire scorches the earth. How would *li* at the South be able to benefit *gen* and *kun*?

8M12: 水冷金寒，坎癸不滋乎乾兌。

When water is cold and metal bitterly so, *gui* at *kan* will not be nourished by *qian* and *dui*.

All *fengshui* systems are derived from the theory of the 5 elements, which generally says that "growth" and "co-prosperous" are desirable, and "control" is not.

Yet 8-Mansions divides the 8 Trigrams into 2 groups, East and West, as follows:

➢ East Group: *kan* (Water), *zhen* and *xun* (Wood) and *li* (Fire), i.e. Water-Wood-Fire "growth" relationships;

➢ West Group: *gen* and *kun* (Earth), *qian* and *dui* (Metal), i.e. Earth-Metal "growth".

What about Fire-Earth and Metal-Water? Surely these too are "growth" relationships, so why is the line of separation drawn right through them?

Lines 8M11 and 8M12 try to justify this separation. Line 8M11 says a hot Fire will scorch the Earth, implying that Fire and Earth should be separated. Likewise, Line 8M12 says cold Metal cannot produce Water, hence they should be separated.

Whether or not one buys this explanation is another matter.

Chapter 2.2: East Group West Group

8M13: 然四卦之互交，固取生旺。

The 4 Trigrams (of each Group) are selected based on their "growth" and "co-prosperous" interactions.

The East and West Group each has 4 Trigrams.

In the East Group, *kan* (Water) grows *zhen* and *xun* (Wood) which in turn grows *li* (Fire). Although Water controls Fire within this group, Wood is present as the mediator. Moreover, Water and Fire do not always fight.

[The classic "Speaking of Hexagrams (說卦傳)" says:

Heaven and Earth set the locations	天地定位
Mountain and Marsh pass the *qi* between them	山澤通氣
Thunder and Wind are mutually attracted	雷風相薄
Water and Fire do not shoot at each other	水火不相射]

It is only when one overwhelms the other that problems will arise.

Hence in an East Group house, the positive Stars: "*sheng qi*", "*tian yi*", "*yan nian*" and "*fu wei*" are always located at the Water, Wood and Fire palaces, i.e. at *kan*, *zhen*, *xun* and *li*.

In the West Group, *gen* and *kun* (Earth) grow *qian* and *dui* (Metal).

Hence in a West Group house, the positive Stars: "*sheng qi*", "*tian yi*", "*yan nian*" and "*fu wei*" are always located at the Earth and Metal palaces, i.e. at *gen*, *kun*, *qian* and *dui*.

All this is elementary 8-Mansions stuff that hardly merits a discussion in our present discourse. However it should be borne in mind that the author Wu Jing Luan (吳景鸞) was first and foremost a *xuan kong* master. To him 8-Mansions was probably a digression that needed to be explained from ground up.

The illogical part is why Master Wu chose to introduce the relatively sophisticated "Star-Palace Interaction" principle first (Lines 8M07, 8M08), and then revert to the basic concept of East and West Groups (Lines 8M11, 8M12, 8M13). Logical presentation does not seem to be a priority with some old texts!

Chapter 2.2: East Group West Group

> **8M14:** 八宮的締合，自有假真。
>
> The associations between the 8 palaces may be real or false.

This line reinforces Line 8M13 above.

The 8 palaces are divided into 2 groups, East and West. Intra-group palaces are mutually supportive, whereas inter-group palaces are mutually antagonistic.

When the palaces are mutually supportive, their associations are said to be "real". Conversely when the palaces are antagonistic, their associations are said to be "false".

8-Mansions requires the door, bed and stove to be located at palaces within the same group. [See Line 8M06 for discussion on stove location] The synergy thus generated will optimize *qi* distribution within the house.

Chapter 2.2: East Group West Group

> **8M15:** 地天爲泰，老陰之土生老陽。
>
> Earth and Heaven make up the "Unity" Hexagram. The Earth of "Old *yin*" (*kun*) grows (the Metal of) Old *yang* (*qian*).

"Earth", "Old *yin*" = *kun*
"Heaven", "Old *yang*" = *qian*

By stacking the Trigam *kun* on top of the Trigram *qian*, we get the Hexagram "Unity (泰)" ☷☰, which represents perfect harmony.

In 8-Mansions language, the Trigrams *kun* and *qian* make up a natural pair: *kun* is *yin* and represents an elderly woman; whereas *qian* is *yang* and represents an elderly man. Both are West Group, and one is the *yan nian* of the other.

yan nian stands for good relationship and harmony. See Appendix-1.

Chapter 2.2: East Group West Group

> **8M16:** 若坤配兌女，庶妾難投寡母之歡心。
>
> If *kun* is matched with *dui*, it is difficult for the subordinate wife to gain the widowed mother's approval.

kun is of Earth element and *dui* is Metal, hence a "growth" relationship. However both *kun* and *dui* are of *yin* polarity, and there is a generation gap. Hence the relationship, though mutually supportive, can also be rather strained.

Further, as both Trigrams are *yin*, the male gender is disadvantaged.

If a *kun* house opens a *dui* door, or vice versa ("*tian yi*"), and the external landforms are oppressive, one can predict that the men folk of the house will be subservient, and in an extreme case, may even suffer an early death – hence the reference to a "widowed mother".

Chapter 2.2: East Group West Group

> **8M17:** 澤山爲咸，少男之情屬少女。
>
> Marsh (*dui*) and Mountain (*gen*) make up the "Influence" hexagram. The young man's feelings belong to the young woman.

The "Influence (咸)" Hexagram is made up of the Trigrams dui ☱ stacked on top of gen, ☶.

In the interpretation of Hexagrams, "Influence" stands for the affections between man and woman.

In 8-Mansions language, the Trigrams *dui* and *gen* make up a natural pair: *dui* is *yin* and represents a girl; whereas *gen* is *yang* and represents a boy. Both are West Group, and one is the *yan nian* of the other.

We have already seen that *yan nian* stands for good relationship and harmony.

Chapter 2.2: East Group West Group

> **8M18:** 若艮配純陽，鰥夫豈有發生之機兆。
>
> If *gen* is matched with the pure *yang* (*qian*), like the widower, there will hardly be an opportunity to procreate.

gen is of Earth element and *qian* is Metal, hence a "growth" relationship. However both *gen* and *qian* are of yang polarity, and there is a generation gap. Hence the relationship, though mutually supportive, lacks the *yin-yang* balance required for growth and sustainability.

As both Trigrams are *yang*, the female gender is disadvantaged.

If a *gen* house opens a *qian* door, or vice versa ("*tian yi*"), and the external landforms are oppressive, one can predict that the women folk of the house will be suppressed, and in an extreme case, may even suffer an early death – hence the reference to a "widower".

Chapter 2.2: East Group West Group

> **8M19:** 乾兌託假鄰之誼；坤艮通偶爾之情。
>
> *qian* and *dui* make insincere neighbours. *kun* and *gen* are affectionate from time to time.

Still on the subject of the 4 West Group Trigrams, Line 8M19 examines the relationships between *qian* and *dui*; *kun* and *gen*.

These pairs are *yin-yang* balanced, and the elements are "co-prosperous" (Metal-Metal, Earth-Earth, respectively). However, there is a generation gap. How long will a relationship between an old man and a young girl last?

The phrases "insincere neighbours" and "affectionate from time to time" both describe impermanent relationships.

In other words, if a *qian* house opens a *dui* door, or vice versa, although it is a "*sheng qi*" door, the benefits will not endure. The same applies to *kun* and *gen*.

Reading from Line 8M15 through to Line 8M19, it is evident that for West Group houses, a "*yan nian*" door is preferred over "*sheng qi*" or "*tian yi*" for procreation and sustainability. "*yan nian*" is a Metal Star and its presence at any of the West Group palaces is harmonious with the palace element (Earth or Metal).

On the other hand, "*sheng qi*" being Wood is hardly comfortable at an Earth or Metal palace. Moreover, there is a generation gap: *qian/dui*; *kun/gen*.

"*tian yi*", though of Earth element, is always uni-polar: *qian/gen*; *kun/dui*, and is thus not conducive to procreation.

Chapter 2.2: East Group West Group

> **8M20:** 雙木成林，雷風相薄。
>
> A pair of wood becomes a forest. Thunder and Wind are mutually attracted.

"A pair of wood" and "Thunder and Wind" refer to the Trigrams *zhen* and *xun*.

zhen and *xun* make up a natural pair: *zhen* is *yang* and represents a middle-aged man; whereas *xun* is *yin* and represents a middle-aged woman. Both are East Group. One is the *yan nian* of the other.

yan nian stands for good relationship and harmony.

Chapter 2.2: East Group West Group

8M21: 中爻得配，水火方交。

The middle line of the Trigrams forms a *yin yang* pair, which is why Water matches well with Fire.

Just a fanciful way to say that *kan* (Water) and *li* (Fire) form a natural pair. *kan* is *yang* and represents a young male adult; whereas *xun* is *yin* and represents a young female adult. Both are East Group. One is the *yan nian* of the other.

As we have seen, *yan nian* stands for good relationship and harmony.

Chapter 2.2: East Group West Group

> **8M22:** 木爲火神之本；水爲木氣之源。
>
> Wood enables Fire, just as Water is the source of Wood.

There are 2 of Wood in 8-Mansions: *zhen* and *xun*, but only 1 each of Fire and Water.

Let us examine each Trigram pair in turn:

- *zhen* Wood and *li* Fire are "growth" and one is the "*sheng qi*" of the other. The 2 Trigrams are also *yin-yang* balanced;

- *xun* Wood and *li* Fire are also "growth" but are both of the *yin* polarity. One is the "*tian yi*" of the other;

- *kan* Water and *zhen* Wood are "growth" but are both *yang*. One is the "*tian yi*" of the other;

- *kan* Water and *xun* Wood are "growth" and are *yin-yang* balanced. One is the "*sheng qi*" of the other.

Chapter 2.2: East Group West Group

8M23: 巽陰就離，風散則火易熄。

xun and *li* are both *yin*. When the Wind scatters, the Fire is easily extinguished.

Although *xun* Wood and *li* Fire enjoy a "growth" relationship, the fact that the Trigrams are both *yin* implies that the benefits tend to be unsustainable.

xun and *li* are "*tian yi*" to each other.

Chapter 2.2: East Group West Group

8M24: 震陽生火，雷奮而火尤明。

zhen is *yang* and grows Fire. Thunder exerts itself and the Fire is especially bright.

zhen Wood and *li* Fire are also "growth", but in addition *zhen* is *yang* and *li* is *yin*. Hence the growth potential is strong and sustainable.

zhen and *li* are "*sheng qi*" to each other.

Chapter 2.2: East Group West Group

> **8M25:** 震與坎爲乍交；離共巽而暫合。
>
> *zhen* and *kan* make fickle acquaintances; *li* and *xun* form a temporary union.

zhen Wood is grown by *kan* Water ("mutual growth"), but both are *yang*.

li Fire is grown by *xun* Wood, but both are *yin*.

In each pair, the Trigrams are "*tian yi*" to each other, but the uni-polar relationships suggest the benefits are not sustainable.

Chapter 2.2: East Group West Group

> **8M26:** 坎元生氣，得巽木而附寵聯歡。
>
> *kan* is the source of "*sheng qi*". Having *xun* Wood will bring about great celebrations.

kan is the "*sheng qi*" of *xun* and vice versa. The Water of *kan* also grows the Wood of *xun*, and the Trigrams are *yin-yang* balanced. Hence to be able to use "*sheng qi*" in a *kan* or *xun* house is especially beneficial.

Reading from Line 8M20 through to Line 8M26, it is evident that "*sheng qi*" and "*yan nian*" are *yin-yang* balanced while "*tian yi*" is not. This statement is equally applicable to East Group and West Group houses.

However, "*sheng qi*" being a Wood Star is more at home in East Group houses than West Group. In East Group houses, "sheng qi" will always be compatible with the palace element (Water, Wood or Fire), which is not the case with West Group.

Moreover, East Group "*sheng qi*" does not suffer from the generation gap problem of West Group [Line 8M19]:

East Group: "*sheng qi*" of *zhen* is *li*, and vice versa, i.e. eldest son paired with middle daughter;

"*sheng qi*" of *xun* is *kan*, and vice versa, i.e. eldest daughter paired with middle son.

West Group: "*sheng qi*" of *qian* is *dui*, and vice versa, i.e. old man with young girl;

"*sheng qi*" of *kun* is *gen*, and vice versa, i.e. old woman with young boy.

That is to say, using "*sheng qi*" in East Group houses has an inherent advantage.

On the other hand, "*yan nian*" being of Metal element tends to be disadvantaged in an East Group house. The only exception is a *li* (South sitting) house, where "*yan nian*" resides at *kan* (Metal-Water growth). Hence a South sitting house has this additional benefit.

Chapter 2.2: East Group West Group

8M27: 乾乏元神，用兌金而傍城借主。

If *qian* (Metal) is lacking its source (Earth), *dui* (Metal) may be used, much like a servant seeking employment from a master in a neighbouring city.

The natural partner of *qian* (Metal) is *kun* (Earth). The 2 Trigrams are ideally matched. [see Line 8M15]

However, if *kun* is unavailable, *dui* (Metal) may also be used. After all *qian-dui* is "co-prosperous", and is *yin-yang* balanced. The only shortcoming is the generation gap (old man and young girl). [see Line 8M19] [I wonder how many times this excuse has been used by an old guy wishing to take on a young mistress/subordinate wife ☺]

For example, it is best for a *qian* house to open a *kun* door ("*yan nian*"), but if that is not possible, a *dui* door ("*sheng qi*") would be next best.

PART-2
"Ode to Mysticism (玄機賦)"
The 8-Mansions Interpretation

Chapter 2.3

Negative Stars

Chapter 2.3
Negative Stars

8M28: 風行地上，決定傷脾。

When Wind traverses the Earth, the spleen will surely be hurt.

Hitherto we have been discussing the relationships between Trigrams within the same Group – East or West.

In this and the next 3 lines, we shall examine inter-group Trigram interactions. This is the territory of the negative "Wandering Stars".

If *xun* (Wind, East Group) is matched with *kun* (Earth, West Group), it is a "*wu gui*" interaction. The Wood of *xun* controls the Earth of *kun*.

kun represents the abdomen and that includes the stomach, spleen and pancreas, as well as the digestive system, muscles, skin, female genitalia, etc.

In other words, having a "*wu gui*" door at a *xun* or *kun* house could bring about *kun* related problems, of which spleen ailment is but one.

Moreover, as the attributes of "*wu gui*" are insidious rather than overtly hostile, we can expect the illness to fester over an extended period rather than a sudden eruption.

Chapter 2.3: Negative Stars

8M29: 火照天門，必當吐血。

When Fire illuminates Heaven's Gate, one will surely vomit blood.

"Fire" = *li*; "Heaven's Gate" = *qian*.

li-qian is a Fire-Metal "control" interaction, and the 2 Trigrams are "*wu gui*" to each other.

As to why the vomiting of blood, the reasoning goes like this: the Trigram *qian* not only represents the head but also the lungs. Traditionally the vomiting of blood is associated with tuberculosis and other lung ailments. Hence when *qian* (Metal) is damaged by *li* (Fire), blood is vomited.

Again, "*wu gui*" suggests that the illness is chronic rather than acute.

In fact, illnesses associated with the head, like migraine, meningitis, stroke, etc. are just as valid diagnoses.

For example, a *qian* house opening a *li* door, or vice versa, would be susceptible.

Landforms that would aggravate the situation include jagged rock faces, power line, microwave transmission tower, tall spire, red building, etc.

Chapter 2.3: Negative Stars

> **8M30:** 木見戌朝，莊生難免鼓盆之嘆。
>
> If Wood (in this case *xun* rather than *zhen*) faces *xu* (*qian*), it will be difficult to avoid the regrettable incident of Zhuang Sheng drumming on a basin.

xun-qian represents a Wood-Metal clash. The 2 Trigrams are "*huo hai*" to each other.

"Zhuang Sheng drumming on a basin" is an idiom meaning the demise of one's wife. See story narrated under Part-1 Line 0M30.

xun (Wood, woman) is severely damaged by *qian* (Metal, man).

The prediction of the wife's death is, in my opinion, unwarranted. After all, "*huo hai*" just stands for obstacles and mishaps, hardly life threatening.

Moreover, "*huo hai*" is an Earth Star. Its presence at *qian* palace (*xun* house) would be "Earth Star residing at Metal palace", a passive situation. Even if "*huo hai*" is present at *xun* palace (*qian* house), the Earth-Wood clash is the least destructive of the 5 elemental clashes. [see Line 8M08]

I think Master Wu simply over-reacted.

Chapter 2.3: Negative Stars

> **8M31:** 坎流坤位，賈臣常遭賤婦之羞。
>
> When water from *kan* flows into *kun*, the humiliation of Jia Chen by his despicable wife will be reenacted.

kan-kun represents a Water-Earth clash. One Trigram is the "*jue ming*" of the other.

The story of "Jia Chen and his despicable wife" is narrated under Part-1 Line OM31.

A *kan* house having a *kun* door, or vice versa, would be susceptible.

kan (Water, man) is controlled by *kun* (Earth, woman) - hence the image of a guy being bullied by his wife, although in the story (Line OM31) the guy got his sweet revenge eventually.

Herein lies the anomaly: whereas Line 8M30 described a "*huo hai*" interaction and the prognosis was death; Line 8M31 here describes a "*jue ming*" interaction which is far more onerous, and the penalty is only divorce.

PART-2
"Ode to Mysticism (玄機賦)"
The 8-Mansions Interpretation

Chapter 2.4
Defective Palaces

Chapter 2.4
Defective Palaces

8M32: 艮非宜也，筋傷股折。

If *gen* is unwell, tendons will be hurt and the thighbone fractures.

This line and the next 2 discuss missing or defective palaces and their effects on the human body.

If *gen* palace is missing or defective, or threatened by negative landforms, the human body parts related to the Trigram *gen* are liable to damage or disease.

The problems could include: fractured limbs; locomotive disorders; rheumatoid arthritis; neurological disorders; etc.

Chapter 2.4: Defective Palaces

8M33: 兌不利歟，唇亡齒寒。

What if *dui* is disadvantaged? The demise of the lips will expose the teeth to bitter cold.

The Trigram *dui* relates to the mouth. A missing or defective *dui* palace aggravated by negative landforms could indicate a cleft lip or other mouth related problems.

Other ailments associated with *dui* include: dental complaints; cough; throat infections; speech impediments; lung infections; menstrual issues; sexually transmitted diseases; knife wounds; etc.

Chapter 2.4: Defective Palaces

> **8M34:** 坎宮缺陷而墮胎；離位巉巖而損目。
>
> A missing or sunken *kan* palace will lead to miscarriage. Jagged rocks at *li* location will impair one's sight.

The Trigram *kan* relates to the following body parts and systems: ears; urinary system; genitals; arteries; intelligence; etc.

When the text says "missing or sunken", it implies a defect with *kan* palace, typically a missing palace or a steep downward slope.

The line mentions miscarriage, but that is only by way of example.

The Trigram *li* relates to the eyes and the heart.

If *li* palace is defective or threatened, such as a jagged rock face outside, then the residents are susceptible to eye and heart ailments.

Exposed rocky cliffs or crumpling rock faces, typically the remnants of quarrying operations or hill cutting by irresponsible developers, are particularly injurious to health.

PART-2
"Ode to Mysticism (玄機賦)"
The 8-Mansions Interpretation

Chapter 2.5

Landform Blessings

Chapter 2.5
Landform Blessings

> **8M35:** 輔臨丁丙，位列朝班。
>
> When "Left & Right Assistant" approaches *bing* and *ding*, one will have a place in the Emperor's morning audience.

"輔 (Assist)" refers to "輔弼 (Left/Right Assistant)", another name for "fu wei".

"*bing* and *ding*" appears to refer to *li* palace which is made up of 3 the sub-sectors: *bing*, *wu* and *ding*.

The straightforward interpretation of Line 8M35 would then be that when "*fu wei*" resides at *li*, members of the household will have a place in the Emperor's morning audience, meaning high office. [See Part-1 Line OM35 for an explanation of the metaphor.]

But then all *li* houses have their "*fu wei*" at *li*. Surely not all these houses are destined to produce ministers? Clearly Master Wu had something else in mind.

I believe he was referring to landforms, i.e. a physical "Left/Right Assistant" mountain at the sub-sectors *bing* and *ding* (15° each).

A "Left/Right Assistant" mountain is a low hill of variable shape, but in this case, Wood shape is best. It is difficult to explain what Wood shape looks like because of its many variations. A pyramid like hill with a blunted peak is Wood shaped, but that is only one specimen. [Please consult landform books for more information.]

The element of "*fu wei*" Star is Wood. The Star represents capable supporters.

Line 8M35 says that if a "Left/Right Assistant" hill is found at the *bing* or *ding* sector of the *luo pan*, measured from the subject property, then the household is likely to produce capable persons who will rise to ministerial (or corporate CEO) status.

Why *bing* and *ding* sectors? That's because at *bing* there is the "Heavenly Noble Star (天貴星)", and at *ding* there is the "Southern Dipper Star (南極星)". Both these Stars in the Southern skies are rated as highly beneficial. In the study of the Heavenly Stars, they are 2 members of the group called the "3 Auspicious 6 Elegance (三吉六秀)".

In terms of elemental interaction, it is Wood growing Fire.

The next 3 lines should also be explained in landform terms.

Chapter 2.5: Landform Blessings

> **8M36:** 巨入坤艮，田連阡陌。
>
> When "Huge Door" enters *kun* and *gen*, farmlands will number in the hundreds and thousands.

"Huge Door (巨門)" is a large rectangular mountain with a flat top. It is of Earth element, and stands for wealth.

If such a mountain is seen at *kun* or *gen* of the *luo pan* (in each case the 15° sub-sector, not the whole palace), then it is a sure sign of landed property wealth.

Why *kun* or *gen*? At *gen* in the Northeastern skies, there is the "Heavenly City Asterism (天市垣)", another member of the "3 Auspicious 6 Elegance (三吉六秀)" group. This asterism is especially good for commerce. [Chinese astrology does not differentiate between asterisms, stars, planets and comets. They are all called "Stars".]

kun is "Mother Earth (地母)". Although there are no beneficial Heavenly Stars of comparable standing at that sector of the Southwestern skies, it benefits from a reflection of the "Heavenly City Asterism" diametrically opposite. Moreover *kun* represents productive land that has an enormous capacity to absorb and produce - hence the prognosis of "hundreds and thousands of farmlands".

In elemental terms, it is Earth co-prospering with Earth.

Chapter 2.5: Landform Blessings

> **8M37:** 名揚科第，貪狼星在巽宮。
>
> When "Greedy Wolf" is located at *xun* palace, one's reputation will spread through the exams.

"Greedy Wolf (貪狼)" is a large Wood shaped mountain. As mentioned earlier (Line 8M35), Wood mountains come in many shapes, from an upright protrusion that looks like one end of a cucumber, to a large pyramid with a rounded top, to an extended protuberance that resembles a flaccid penis… Such a mountain is of the Wood element, and stands for nobility, high status, and helpful persons.

At the *xun* (15°) sector of the Southeastern skies, there is the "Greater Covert Asterism (太微垣)", a very noble Star that represents high office. In addition to being a member of the "3 Auspicious 6 Elegance (三吉六秀)" group, it is also one of the "Heavenly Stars 4 Nobles (天星四貴)".

Hence if a "Greedy Wolf" mountain is seen outside *xun* palace, it is as if the "Greater Covert Asterism" has landed, bringing with it the status and spoils of high office.

In elemental terms, it is Wood co-prospering with Wood.

Chapter 2.5: Landform Blessings

> **8M37:** 職掌兵權，武曲峰當庚兌。
>
> When a "Military Arts" mountain matches with *geng* and *dui*, military power will be to hand.

"Military Arts (武曲)" is a relatively low bun shaped hill. It signals military power, and in modern society, executive authority and responsibility.

At the *geng* sector of the Western skies, there is the "Military Baron (武爵)" Star; and at *dui* (in the present context read as *you*) there is the "Lesser Covert Asterism (少微垣)", another of the "3 Auspicious 6 Elegance (三吉六秀)" and "Heavenly Stars 4 Nobles (天星四貴)".

If a "Military Arts" mountain is seen outside *geng* or *you*, the Star's influence is greatly amplified by the landform.

In elemental terms, it is Metal co-prospering with Metal.

PART-2
"Ode to Mysticism (玄機賦)"
The 8-Mansions Interpretation

Chapter 2.6
Body Parts

Chapter 2.6
Body Parts

8M39: 乾首坤腹，八卦推詳。

qian represents the head and *kun* the belly. Such associations may be derived from the 8 Trigrams.

8M40: 癸足丁心，十干類取。

gui represents the feet and *ding* the heart. Such associations may be obtained from the 10 stems.

These 2 lines point out that the human body parts are associated with certain Trigrams and Heavenly Stems (and by implication also Earthly Branches), and ailments of these body parts are often reflected in defects of these Metaphysical entities, such as an elemental clash or the presence of negative landforms.

In this respect, there is no difference between the 8-Mansions interpretation and that of *xuan kong*. [See Part-1 Lines OM39, OM40]

PART-2
"Ode to Mysticism (玄機賦)"
The 8-Mansions Interpretation

Chapter 2.7
East/West Differences

Chapter 2.7
East/West Differences

8M41: 木入坎宮，鳳池身貴。

Wood entering *kan* palace provides one with high enough status to be admitted to the "Phoenix Pool".

On the surface, this line says when the "*sheng qi*" Star (Wood) enters *kan* (Water) palace, the residents will enjoy high status.

"Phoenix Pool" is a metaphor implying high society. [See Part-w Line OM41 for an explanation]

Now the "*sheng qi*" of a *xun* house is located at *kan*. So does it mean all *xun* houses are destined for high society? Clearly not so.

It behooves us to take a broader view: "Wood entering *kan* palace" points to a "growth" interaction that is also *yin-yang* balanced for East Group houses. East Group "*sheng qi*" satisfies these conditions:

➢ *kan* house has "*sheng qi*" at *xun* – Water-Wood "growth", *yin-yang* balanced;

➢ *xun* house has "*sheng qi*" at *kan* – same;

➢ *zhen* house has "*sheng qi*" at *li* – Wood-Fire "growth", *yin-yang* balanced;

➢ *li* house has "*sheng qi*" at *zhen* – same.

Line 8M41 therefore implies that for East Group houses having a "*sheng qi*" door, the road to success tends to be through the established route. In the old days, that would mean studying hard, passing the exams, entering the civil service, promotion through the ranks, getting to rub shoulders with the high and mighty, etc.

In modern society, that would equate to going to university, getting a good degree and a steady job, gradual promotions to senior executive levels, share options, golf clubs, social fraternities, public awards, etc.

After all, the elements Water, Wood and Fire relate to intelligence, progress and elegance.

The road to success is markedly different for West Group houses.

Chapter 2.7: East/West Differences

> **8M42:** 金居艮位，烏府求名。
>
> Metal occupying *gen* location represents a person seeking a position at the "House of Ravens".

On the surface, the line says that when the "*yan nian*" Star (Metal) enters *gen* (Earth) palace, the residents will also attain high positions, but through a different route.

The metaphor "House of Ravens" refers to high government office. [See Part-1 Line OM42]

Now the "*yan nian*" of a *dui* house is located at *gen*. So does it mean all *dui* houses will produce high level officials? That would be unrealistic.

Like the previous line, "Metal occupying *gen* location" merely points to a "growth" interaction that is also *yin-yang* balanced for West Group houses. West Group "*yan nian*" satisfies these conditions:

➢ *gen* house has "*yan nian*" at *dui* – Metal-Earth "growth", *yin-yang* balanced;

➢ *dui* house has "*yan nian*" at *gen* – same;

➢ *kun* house has "*yan nian*" at *qian* – same;

➢ *qian* house has "*yan nian*" at *kun* – same.

Line 8M42 therefore implies that for West Group houses having a "*yan nian*" door, the road to success tends to be through the so-called "alternative" route. In the old days, that could mean a military career, or doing well in business and buying oneself a position in the civil service.

[Whilst the latter may sound unsavory (but not unheard of) today, the practice was socially acceptable in the old days. They even had a polite name for it: "donate to a position (捐官)"]

In modern society, there are many equivalents. Any means to public recognition, other than through the "straight and narrow", could be considered an "alternative" route. Some are no less honourable.

After all, the elements Earth and Metal relate to trust, wealth and decisiveness, including an element of force if needed.

Chapter 2.7: East/West Differences

> **8M43:** 金取土培，火宜木相。
>
> Metal seeks the nourishment of Earth, just as Fire desires the companionship of Wood.

This line restates what is implied in Lines 8M41 and 8M42 above, that there are significant differences between East Group and West Group houses. Note that the Wood-Fire interaction is mentioned here in place of Water-Wood earlier. Both are East Group. This could be a hint by Master Wu that the reader should not take the lines at face value but probe deeper.

Read in this way, the line serves as a summary that 8-Mansions is all about East Group and West Group. In East Group houses, the 4 beneficial "Wandering Stars" ("*sheng qi*", "*tian yi*", "*yan nian*", "*fu wei*") are distributed between the Water/Wood/Fire palaces; whereas in West Group houses, these 4 beneficial Stars are to be found at the Earth/Metal palaces. It follows that the key features of a house, namely the door, bed and stove, should be located differently according to East Group/West Group.

To borrow from the words of Rudyard Kipling, "Oh, East is East and West is West, and never the twain shall meet." [Was Kipling ever a *fengshui* master? ☺]

Line 8M43 therefore makes more sense as a closing line in this 8-Mansions interpretation of the poem "Ode to Mysticism (玄機賦)". In the *xuan kong* version, the final line appears to have left the poem dangling in mid-air.

Moreover, the lines on the whole appear to be better laid out in the 8-Mansions version. The flow of ideas is perceptibly smoother, minor diversions notwithstanding. The flow is a lot more disjointed in the *xuan kong* version.

So was Wu Jing Luan (吳景鸞) enough of a maverick to sing an 8-Mansions song to a *xuan kong* tune, and have a good laugh over it? ☺☺ Let the reader be the judge.

APPENDICES

Appendix-1:
"Wandering Stars"

Appendix-1
"Wandering Stars"

The 8-Mansions system is made up of 2 sets of Metaphysical entities: the 8 Trigrams (卦) and the 8 "Wandering Stars (遊星)". All discussions on 8-Mansions are hinged on these 2 parameters.

I trust there is no need to introduce the 8 Trigrams. Fig-A101 sets out the 2 different arrangements, dubbed "Early Heaven (先天)" and "Later Heaven (後天)".

"Early Heaven" arrangement   "Later Heaven" arrangement

Fig-A101: 8 Trigrams

Theoretically, the "Wandering Stars" are derived from a process of Trigram transformation called the "Greater Wandering Years Trigram Transformation (大遊年翻卦)", but we shall not bother with that here. Instead we shall take a graphical approach, starting with the Early Heaven arrangement of the 8 Trigrams.

Fig-A102 is a graphical representation of the 4 auspicious "Wandering Stars (遊星)" in terms of their Trigram relationships. Each of the diagrams is basically the Early Heaven arrangement of the 8 Trigrams, superimposed with the *luo shu* numbers 1 to 9, except that #5 at the centre has been omitted for clarity.

Appendix-1: "Wandering Stars"

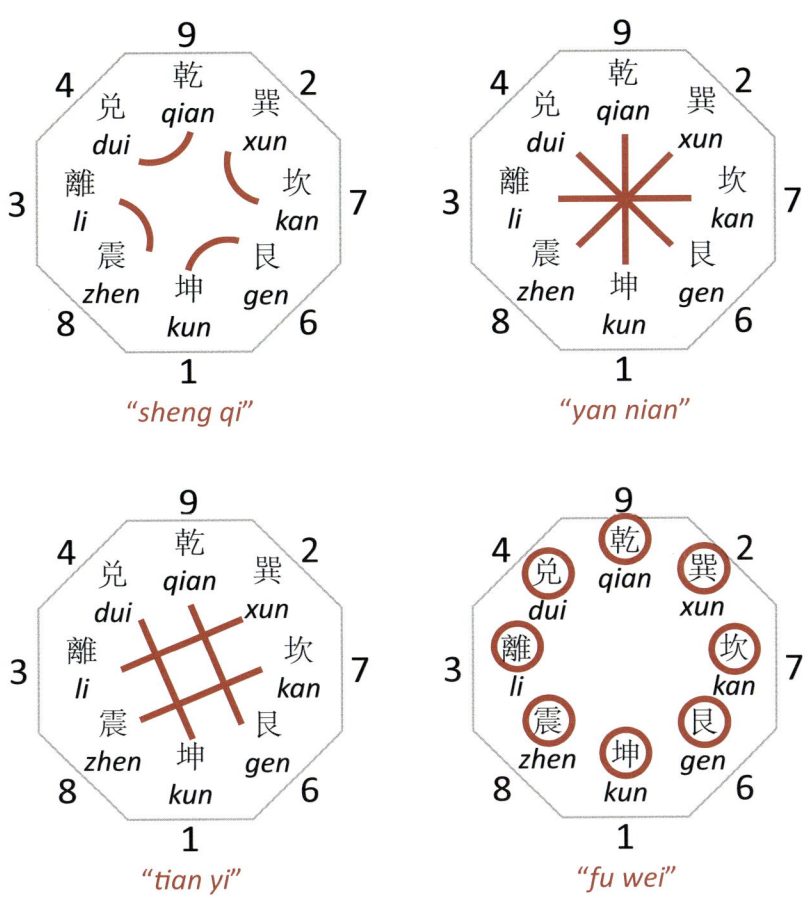

Fig-A102: 4 auspicious Wandering Stars

When the *luo shu* numbers of a pair of Trigrams match with the so-called "Birth and Completion Numbers (生成數)" (1-6; 2-7; 3-8, 4-9), then one Trigram of the pair is the "*sheng qi*" of the other: eg. *kun* is the "*sheng qi*" of *gen* and vice versa; *xun* is the "*sheng qi*" of *kan* and vice versa. "Birth and Completion Numbers" are sometimes called "*he tu* (河圖) Combinations".

When the *luo shu* numbers of a pair of Trigrams add up to 10 (1-9; 2-8; 3-7; 4-6), then one Trigram of the pair is the "*yan nian*" of the other: eg. *qian* is the "*yan nian*" of *kun* and vice versa; *xun* is the "*yan nian*" of *zhen* and vice versa. These pairs are sometimes called "Combinations of 10 (合十數)" or "Later Heaven Combinations".

Appendix-1: "Wandering Stars"

When the *luo shu* numbers of a pair of Trigrams add up to 5 or 15 (1-4; 2-3; 6-9; 7-8), then one Trigram of the pair is the "*tian yi*" of the other: eg. *kun* is the "*tian yi*" of *dui* and vice versa; *zhen* is the "*tian yi*" of *kan* and vice versa.

"*fu wei*" is simply the Trigram itself: i.e. the "*fu wei*" of *li* is *li*; the "*fu wei*" of *kan* is *kan*.

Fig-A102 demonstrates that the principles of 8-Mansions are founded on the Early Heaven arrangement of the 8 Trigrams, even though the Later Heaven arrangement is commonly used when we describe the 8 palaces (eg. *qian* at NW, *kun* at SW, etc. See Fig-A101). This is one manifestation of the popular saying "Early Heaven becomes the body, Later Heaven the application (先天爲體，後天爲用)".

Fig-A103 sets out the 4 inauspicious "Wandering Stars" in the same manner as in Fig-A102, but the associated *luo shu* numbers do not add up quite as elegantly.

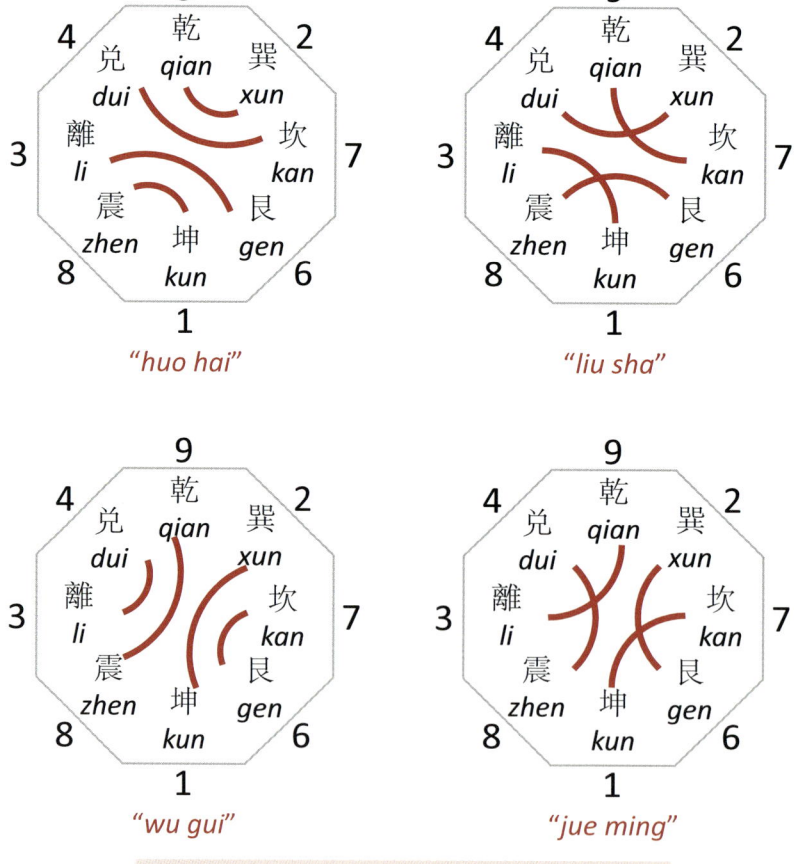

Fig-A103: 4 inauspicious Wandering Stars

Appendix-1: "Wandering Stars"

In what ways are the "auspicious" Stars beneficial, and the "inauspicious" Stars harmful? That's determined by their attributes, as summarized in the following table. In addition, each "Wandering Star" is assigned an element, the significance of which will become clear when we use the Stars in the different palaces.

Wandering Star		element	attributes
fu wei (伏位)	[beneficial]	*yin* Wood	stability, self cultivation
sheng qi (生氣)	[beneficial]	*yang* Wood	vibrant energy, financial gains
wu gui (五鬼)	[harmful]	Fire	betrayal, petty people
yan nian (延年)	[beneficial]	*yang* Metal	relationships, harmony
liu sha (六殺)	[harmful]	Water	injury, arguments
huo hai (禍害)	[harmful]	*yin* Earth	obstacles, mishaps
tian yi (天醫)	[beneficial]	*yang* Earth	good health, helpful people
jue ming (絕命)	[harmful]	*yin* Metal	life threatening, financial ruin

In all schools of *fengshui*, and indeed in almost every branch of Chinese Metaphysics, a collection of stars called the "Big Dipper Asterism (北斗星)" in the Northern skies plays centre stage. 8-Mansions is no exception. The 8 "Wandering Stars" are inexorably linked to the stars of the "Big Dipper", even though the "Wandering Stars" are virtual entities whereas the "Big Dipper" Stars are real stellar bodies.

In modern astronomical language, the "Big Dipper" is an asterism (arbitrary collection of stars) within the constellation Ursa Major (Great Bear). The linkages between the Wandering Stars and the North Dipper stars are tabulated below:

Wandering Stars	North Dipper Stars		
	Chinese Name	Greek Name	Modern Ref.
sheng qi (生氣)	Greedy Wolf (貪狼)	Dubhe	αUMa
tian yi (天醫)	Huge Door (巨門)	Merak	βUMa
huo hai (禍害)	Rewards (祿存)	Phecda	γUMa
liu sha (六殺)	Literary Arts (文曲)	Megrez	δUMa
wu gui (五鬼)	Chastity (廉貞)	Alioth	εUMa
yan nian (延年)	Military Arts (武曲)	Mizar	ζUMa
jue ming (絕命)	Broken Soldier (破軍)	Alkaid	ηUMa
fu wei (伏位)	Left Assistant (左輔) & Right Assistant (右弼)	Alcor (none)	80UMa M101

Appendix-1: "Wandering Stars"

But according to the Chinese astronomers the "North Dipper" has 9 Stars, whereas there are only 8 "Wandering Stars". To overcome that anomaly, 8-Mansions assigned both the "Left Assistant" and "Right Assistant" to "*fu wei*".

from the ramblings of one hhc, a fengshui crazee
Feb-2011

> *The ancient Chinese astronomers mapped the skies in detail as early as 1000 BCE. According to them, there were 9 stars in the "Big Dipper (北斗星)".*
>
> *The ancient Greeks were also great astronomers, but they saw only 8 stars.*
>
> *The 9th star, which the Chinese called "Right Assistant (右弼)" was not visible to the naked eye. So how did the ancients know about its existence? That we'll never know for sure.*
>
> *Modern astronomers postulated that the Chinese were referring to a distant galaxy within the constellation Ursa Major, discovered in 1781 with the aid of powerful telescopes, and subsequently named M101.*

Appendix-2:
"Star-Palace Interaction"

Appendix-2
"Star-Palace Interaction"

This is an article I first published in the Web back in 2006. The feedback suggested the readers liked it. Since then, my understanding of 8-Mansions has improved, and some of the issues discussed may no longer be moot, but I decided to reproduce the article intact anyway.

There is no need to read this Appendix to be able to understand the discussions in this book, but readers who wish to probe deeper into 8-Mansions will certainly find it useful.

Many students may be under the impression that the popular "8-Mansions Bright Mirror (八宅明鏡)" is the be-all-and-end-all of 8-Mansions. Even if the article only manages to dispel that notion and broaden their awareness to other equally noteworthy 8-Mansions texts, it would have achieved much.

So here goes…

O' Astral Wanderer, take heed whither ye alight...

Preamble

Location location location, that's the battle cry of today's real estate business. Interestingly the same could have been an issue with the Wandering Stars of 8-Mansions *fengshui*, albeit in a different context. ☺

Of late much interest has been expressed in the Mastery Community, under various forums, on the interplay of elements between the Wandering Stars and the Palaces they visit. The discussions prompted me to look up what the classical texts and other writers have to say, and in the process unearthed a plethora of divergent interpretations. I am happy to share my findings herein, and in the concluding paragraphs, table my own view and the reasoning behind.

As this paper is an attempt, feeble as it may be, at academic research, I dearly welcome comments and criticisms, all in the spirit of advancing our knowledge of 8-Mansions *fengshui*. Chinese writers are fond of using the phrase "throw out a brick to attract jade (拋磚引玉)". Whilst this may be labeled "unrealistic profit expectations" in today's world, it's a nice thought. ☺

The classical name of the topic being discussed is "*gong xing sheng ke*" (宮星生剋), which may be simply translated as "elemental interplay between Palace and Star".

Appendix-2: "Star-Palace Interaction"

Background

Whereas the 8 Wandering Stars: *sheng qi*, *tian yi*, *yan nian*, *fu wei*, *huo hai*, *liu sha*, *wu gui* and *jue ming* are invariably taught in all study courses on 8-Mansions, much less is said about the Stars' intrinsic elements, and how the interplay between the visiting Star and the host Palace will affect the strength of the Star.

The 8 Wandering Stars, the heavenly stars associated with them, their respective metaphysical elements and polarity are tabulated below:

Wandering Star (遊星)	Heavenly Star (天星)	Element	Polarity
sheng qi (生氣)	Greedy Wolf (貪狼)	Wood	*yang*
tian yi (天醫)	Hugh Door (巨門)	Earth	*yang*
yan nian (延年)	Military Arts (武曲)	Metal	*yang*
fu wei (伏位)	Left Assistant (左輔)	Wood	*yin*
huo hai (禍害)	Rewards (祿存)	Earth	*yin*
liu sha (六煞)	Literary Arts (文曲)	Water	*yang*
wu gui (五鬼)	Chastity (廉貞)	Fire	*yin*
jue ming (絕命)	Broken Soldier (破軍)	Metal	*yin*

The first 4 (*sheng qi, tian yi, yan nian, fu wei*) are the good guys, and the other 4 the baddies. That's common knowledge, but how good or how bad? That will depend on where the Star lands in the *luo shu* (洛書) chart, i.e. which Palace. The extent to which the Palace, as host, affects the Star, as visitor, is open to interpretation, and opinions do diverge widely between writers.

The *luo shu* Palaces need no introduction, but the following table is included for easy reference:

Location	*luo shu* Number	Palace Name	Element	Polarity
Northwest	6	*qian* (乾)	Metal	*yang*
North	1	*kan* (坎)	Water	*yang*
Northeast	8	*gen* (艮)	Earth	*yang*
East	3	*zhen* (震)	Wood	*yang*
West	7	*dui* (兌)	Metal	*yin*
Southwest	2	*kun* (坤)	Earth	*yin*
South	9	*li* (離)	Fire	*yin*
Southeast	4	*xun* (巽)	Wood	*yin*

Appendix-2: "Star-Palace Interaction"

This is what the classics, and other masters more learned than I, have to say:

8-Mansions Bright Mirror (八宅明鏡):

Probably the best known of the 8-Mansions classics, the work is often attributed to the Taoist monk Ruo Guan (箬冠道師) who lived in the early Qing Dynasty. The version that survived has a preface dated 1790 in which the writer said he obtained a copy from Ruo, but did not say Ruo actually wrote it.

> [QUOTE]
>
> ... Palace is internal, Star external. Partially negative if internal counters external, totally negative if external counters internal. *yang* Star countering *yin* Palace will harm females, whereas *yin* Star countering *yang* Palace will harm males. Example: if Rewards *yin* earth Star enters Kan, a *yang* (water) Palace denoting the middle male, the latter is affected negatively...
>
> Greedy Wolf... is in positive territory at *kan*, *li*, *zhen* and *xun*. At *qian* and *dui*, it is countered internally and turns negative. At *kun* and *gen*, it is engaged in battle and its benevolence is reduced...
>
> Hugh Door... in positive territory at *qian*, *dui*, *kun* and *li*... countered internally at *zhen* and *xun*... external battle at *kan*...
>
> Military Arts... in positive territory at *qian*, *dui*, *gen* and *kun*... countered internally at *li*... external battle at *zhen* and *xun*...
>
> [/QUOTE]

Note that "Bright Mirror" appears to have contradicted itself. The first paragraph says Star countering Palace is more onerous, whereas the later paragraphs say otherwise.

We can summarize "Bright Mirror's" stand as follows:

1. If the Palace grows the Star, or the Star grows the Palace, or the elements are mutually supportive (same), a positive Star stays positive;

2. If a negative Star enters a Palace of opposite polarity, the family member associated with the Palace is affected negatively.

"Bright Mirror" does not address the following issues:

1. What if a negative Star enters a Palace that grows, or is grown by, or supports the Star's element? Will the negative Star flex its negative muscles more vigorously, or will it become more civil in a harmonious environment?

2. What about negative Star and Palace having the same polarity? Will the associated family member be affected?

Appendix-2: "Star-Palace Interaction"

Golden Light Star Arrivals Classic (金光斗臨經)

Written by Jin Wen Rong (金文鎔) and first published in 1779, this is another Qing Dynasty classic that is often regarded, jointly with "Bright Mirror", as the definitive manuals of 8-Mansions *fengshui*. The 2 classics cover much common ground (wonder who copied from whom?), except "Golden Light" makes more use of case studies. Surprisingly I am unable to find in "Golden Light" any meaningful discussion on elemental interplay between Palace and Star.

3 Essentials of *yang* Dwellings (陽宅三要)

Written by Zhao Jiu Feng (趙九峰) in 1786, the book is of the same genre as "Bright Mirror" and "Golden Light" although its treatment of Star distribution differs. In terms of elemental interplay between Palace and Star, "3 Essentials" has this to say:

> [QUOTE]
>
> *sheng qi* is of Wood element: it occupies its rightful locations at *zhen*, *xun*, *kan* and *li* palaces, and gives rise to exalted wealth and nobility. 5 sons will be born. The benefits will be realized during *jia*, *yi*, *hai*, *mao*, *wei* years. Especially beneficial to the eldest son.
>
> *tian yi* of Earth element occupies its rightful locations at *kun*, *gen*, *qian* and *dui* palaces, and gives rise to good fortune, wealth and nobility, compassion and benevolence. 3 sons are born. Benefits realizable in *wu*, *ji*, *chen* and *wei* years. Especially beneficial to the middle son.
>
> *yan nian* of Metal element occupies its rightful locations at *qian*, *kun*, *gen* and *dui* palaces, and bestows military powers, produces heroes and public idols. 4 sons are born. Benefits realizable in *geng*, *xin*, *si*, *you* and *chou* years. Especially beneficial to the young sons.
>
> *wu gui* of Fire element is a major negative star responsible for ghostly occurrences, legal suits, slander, gossip, fire and robbery. 2 sons are born. Harmful effects manifested in *bing*, *ding*, *yin*, *wu* and *xu* years. Bad for the eldest son.
>
> *huo hai* of Earth element produces deaf, dumb and blind persons, orphans, widows, poverty and hardship, but long life. Bad for the youngest son.
>
> Literary Arts (*liu sha*) of Water element is responsible for licentious and scandalous behaviour, death by hanging, dispersal of wealth. 1 son is born.
>
> *jue ming* of Metal element is a major negative star that causes serious illnesses, premature death, lack of descendants, orphans, widows and bankruptcies.
>
> [/QUOTE]

The above thoughts are not unique to "3 Essentials". The author merely echoed similar passages found in other Qing Dynasty and earlier 8-Mansions books.

Appendix-2: "Star-Palace Interaction"

Collection of Classics on the Physiognomy of Dwellings (相宅經纂)

Purportedly written by Yi Xing the Monk (一行僧), the venerable Tang Dynasty scholar monk and astronomer, as early as AD632, this collection of papers was edited and re-published in 1844 during the *Qing* Dynasty. It is a noteworthy precursor to "Bright Mirror".

[QUOTE]

... Greedy Wolf resides at the North, owner prosperous. Hugh Door arrives at Fire (South), descendents strong. Military Arts best at Earth locations (Northeast, Southwest). Each residing at its home location is also beneficial (GW at E & SE, etc). Only for *liusha* Literary Arts Water, the Central Palace being countered is not harmful (meaning unclear)...

Greedy Wolf prospers the eldest son, Hugh Door the middle son. Military Arts enriches the youngest son. Literary Arts spoils the middle son, as does Rewards the youngest son. Broken Soldier and Chastity impoverish the eldest son...

Greedy Wolf (Wood Star) should not enter *qian* or *dui* (Metal Palaces), the eldest son dies young, the old man is harmed. Abundant fields and silk worms but nobody to manage them. The widow watches over an empty house.

Hugh Door and Rewards (Earth Stars) should not enter *zhen* or *xun* (Wood Palaces) the family fortune will be diminished first and then the old man harmed. Hugh Door entering *zhen* brings death to the middle son; Rewards entering *xun* hurts the women folk.

Literary Arts (Water Star) should not enter *gen* or *kun* (Earth Palaces), the women and the old man will be harmed most. *gen* countering Literary Arts will harm the male; whereas *kun* countering Literary Arts will harm the women.

Chastity (Fire Star) entering *kan* (Water Palace), the home of water, will lead to death by drowning in a well or river, and missing presumed dead. The eldest son loses his mind amongst thieves and robbers. Soldiers suffer a painful death under the knife and sword.

Military Arts and Broken Soldier (Metal Stars) entering *li* (Fire Palace) leads to difficult births, diseases and ill-fated deaths. Military Arts being countered spoils the youngest son; Broken Soldier being countered impacts the eldest son negatively.

Left and Right Assistants (Wood Star) entering *qian* or *dui* (Metal Palaces) cause the family size and fortune to dwindle over time.

The Central Palace is the most dangerous, requiring the old mother to take control of family matters (implying the males have all died, but relevance unclear)...

... Positive for *yannian* Military Arts Metal to reside at the West, and negative for *tianyi* Hugh Door Earth to sit East. *wugui* Chastity fears *kan*, *qian* and *dui*, never positive. *liusha* Literary Arts worries about *kun*, *gen* and *li*, always negative. Military Arts and Broken Soldier regard *zhen*, *xun* and *li* as their nemeses. Greedy Wolf is the enemy of *kun*, *gen* and the Central Palace. He who is grown prospers; he who is countered dies... He who does battle turns negative; he who receives support stays positive...

[/QUOTE]

Appendix-2: "Star-Palace Interaction"

Physiognomy of Dwellings' position may be summarized as follows:

1. The positive Stars (Greedy Wolf, Huge Door, Military Arts) impact the family members associated with them positively or negatively depending on whether the Star enters a friendly or hostile Palace. In this context, Greedy Wolf impacts the eldest son, Huge Door the middle son and Military Arts the youngest son;

2. The negative Stars Broken Soldier and Chastity harm the eldest son, whereas Literary Arts injures the middle son, and Rewards the youngest son;

   (We know that Palaces have family members associated with them. Now it appears Stars too have their favorite sons.)

3. Stars do not like to counter or be countered by the Palaces;

4. The only favorable situations are when the Palace grows or supports the positive Star. Nothing is said about the negative Stars being grown or supported;

5. From the semantics, it is evident this classic considers the situation of Palace countering Star more onerous than the other way around.

The Complete Book of 8-Mansions Techniques (八宅造福周書)

Written by Huang Yi Feng (黃一鳳), circa 1610, this is a pre-Qing Dynasty book on 8-Mansions. Old books like this remind us that the Qing Dynasty writings, popular as they are, do not have monopoly in dictating 8-Mansions tenets. The book has some interesting things to say about Stars and Palaces.

> [QUOTE]
>
> ... Palace can mean a door, house or room. Star refers to the 3 positive Stars *sheng qi*, *tian yi* and *yan nian*, and the 4 negative Stars *jue ming*, *wu gui*, *huo hai* and *liu sha*. When a Stars flies into a mutual growth Palace or a mutually supportive Palace, then a positive Star becomes more positive, and a negative Star becomes less negative. It's like a malicious person becoming more civil and less inclined to cause trouble. If the Star and Palace counter each other, then positive loses its positive nature, and negative becomes even more negative. In this case, Star countering Palace is worse than Palace countering Star. Palace is the host, and Star the guest. It is permissible for the host to triumph over the guest, but not for the guest to intimidate the host...
>
> [/QUOTE]

Huang takes the view that a negative Star becomes less negative in a growth or supportive environment.

Huang considers it less serious for the host Palace to counter the guest Star.

Note the use of the term "loses its positive nature". Does that mean becoming negative or just neutral?

Appendix-2: "Star-Palace Interaction"

Simple 8-Mansions *fengshui* (易學易用八宅風水)

This is an entry level book on 8-Mansions *fengshui* by the Hong Kong master and prolific writer Bai He Ming (白鶴鳴), first published in 1996. It is not meant to be an academic treatise, but the writing style is clear, concise and easily understood.

> [QUOTE]
>
> ... Every Star is affected by the element of the Palace it enters, and the Star's positive or negative character is enhanced or reduced, according to the general theory of interactions between elements.
>
> For example, if the *sheng qi* Star of a *qian* house or *qian* person enters *dui* Palace, and as *sheng qi* is of Wood element whereas *dui* is Metal, the benevolent *sheng qi* Star is countered by the Palace element, and that reduces its benevolence.
>
> Another example: the negative *jue ming* Star of a *kun* house or *kun* person enters *kan* Palace. *jue ming* Star is Metal, whereas *kan* Palace is Water. As the *jue ming* Star is being depleted, its capacity to do harm is diminished.
>
> In general, positive Stars entering favorable Palaces (being grown or supported) will become more positive, and conversely if they enter unfavorable Palaces (being countered or depleted) they will become less positive. Likewise, negative Stars entering favorable Palaces (being grown or supported) will become more negative, and in unfavorable Palaces (being countered or depleted), their capacity to do harm will be reduced. This concept is similar to the strength of stars in different palaces according to Purple Star destiny analysis...
>
> [/QUOTE]

In addition, the author drew up a chart showing the varying strengths of the 8 Wandering Stars in different Palaces. In the chart he indicated a Star countering the Palace element as being neutral, and said the Star is not much affected. This view is unique.

The author went on to detail the steps a student should take in assessing the effect of the Wandering Stars:

> [QUOTE]
>
> 1. The reader should first understand the intrinsic positive or negative nature of each Star. This is very important. A positive Star will always be a positive Star. Under no circumstances will it turn negative. Likewise, a negative Star is always a negative Star. It cannot turn positive;
>
> 2. Examine the distribution of 8-Mansions Wandering Star map of the house. Study the interplay between the Star's intrinsic element and the Palace element in each Palace to evaluate the relative strength of the Stars;
>
> 3. Consider the timeliness of the Stars according to the Stems and Branches of years and months to predict when the positive or negative nature of a particular Star is likely to strike.
>
> [/QUOTE]

Appendix-2: "Star-Palace Interaction"

Bai's view is simply and clearly stated. Some of his interpretations are fairly novel, for instance, the introduction of a 'neutral' state. In the old classics, it's either positive or negative and nothing in between. Bai's assertion that a positive Star cannot turn negative is very logical. However, his reference to Purple Star principles runs contrary to what I've been taught: according to the Zhong Zhou School (中州派) of Purple Star destiny analysis, a negative Star entering a harmonious Palace will be placated and hence behave relatively well, whereas the same Star entering a hostile Palace will turn rebellious and ferocious.

Bai's approach casts the Star as the main player, i.e. the effect of the Palace element on the Star element is paramount.

Point No. 3 will be discussed later under "The Time Dimension".

Mastery Journal Vol-2 Issue-9, 29-Oct-2004

That issue carried an article by Master Jayne Goodrick entitled "Elementally, My Dear Boy!"

Master Jayne takes the view that a negative Star (*jue ming* in her example) will be less damaging when it is supported by the Palace (*dui*), than would be the case if the Star were to land at a hostile Palace (*zhen*).

Debating Various Aspects of *yang* Dwellings (陽宅諸說辨正)

This book by Taiwanese master Xie Ming Rui (謝明瑞), published in 2001, sets out to explain/argue various teachings of *yang* house *fengshui*. On the topic of elemental interplay between Palace and Star, the author has this to say:

> [QUOTE]
>
> ... What is meant by elemental interplay? If Palace and Star are both *yin*, their elements are also *yin*, or if they are all *yang*, like *tian yi* and *yan nian* are both *yang* and their Palaces are also *yang*, then even if the elements counter each other, the issue of elemental interplay does not arise. Such a situation is called "Palace and Star walking the same path" (宮星同道).
>
> Elemental interplay only comes into being when opposite polarities counter each other. For example, *sheng qi* is *yang* Wood. A *gen gua* person has *kun* as his *sheng qi*. In this case a *yang* Wood Star counters the *yin* Earth of *kun* Palace. Star countering Palace is called external countering internal.
>
> Another example: a *qian gua* person has his *sheng qi* at *dui*. *shengqi* is *yang* Wood, whereas *dui* Palace is *yin* Metal. This case of *yin* Metal countering *yang* Wood is called Palace countering Star, or internal countering external. Half negative.
>
> In the case of a *yang* house sitting *kun* facing *gen*, and the owner is a West group person of *gen gua*, *kun* is by right his *sheng qi*, but *sheng qi* is *yang* Wood and *kun* Palace is *yin* Earth. *yang* Wood countering *yin* Earth at a *yin* Palace is called external

Appendix-2: "Star-Palace Interaction"

> countering internal, which is totally negative...
>
> If a *gen* sitting house opens the main door at its *sheng qi* location *kun*, the *yin* Earth of *kun* is countered by *sheng qi's yang* Wood. As *kun* represents the spleen and stomach, these organs are prone to illness, and the victim will be the mother as *kun* also represents the mother. If the stove is turned to face *qian*, then the severity will be lessened, as *qian* is *tian yi* to *gen*.
>
> [/QUOTE]

2 points stand out:

1. The issue of polarity has now surfaced. We are told that the whole matter of elemental interplay between Palace and Star only applies if the Palace and Star are of opposite polarities;

2. Xie rates Star countering Palace (so-called external) as being more onerous than Palace countering Star (so-called internal).

Website www.fengshui-chinese.com (術數縱橫網頁**)**

The owner of the website posted an interesting article on this topic in Nov-2004. Briefly, his stand on the matter is:

1. Palace countering Star, so-called "internal", is more damaging than Star countering Palace, so-called "external". However, the author makes the point that both cases are negative;

2. A *yang* Star entering a *yang* Palace, and likewise a *yin* Star entering a *yin* Palace, are excluded from elemental interplay considerations. It's called "Palace and Star walking the same path";

3. Only when a Star enters a Palace of the opposite polarity is it necessary to invoke the elemental interplay (growth/counter) issue.

The polarity issue also surfaces here.

The author goes on to list the positive and negative Palaces for each of the 8 house *gua* after accounting for elemental interplay. The conclusion is that only *dui*, *xun* and *kun* houses manage to retain 4 favorable Palaces; *kan*, *zhen*, *li* houses are left with 3; whereas *qian* and *gen* houses have only 2 favorable Palaces left. House hunters beware.

Appendix-2: "Star-Palace Interaction"

The Time Dimension

When would a Wandering Star, positive or negative, be most likely to manifest its attributes?

There seems to be fairly universal agreement on the Wood, Metal, Water and Fire Stars:

Wandering Star	Most active years, months
sheng qi Greedy Wolf (Wood) *fu wei* Left/Right Assistants (Wood)	*hai* (亥), *mao* (卯), *wei* (未), *jia* (甲), *yi* (乙)
yan nian Military Arts (Metal) *jue ming* Broken Soldier (Metal)	*si* (巳), *you* (酉), *chou* (丑), *geng* (庚), *xin* (辛)
liu sha Literary Arts (Water)	*shen* (申), *zi* (子), *chen* (辰), *ren* (壬), *gui* (癸)
wu gui Chastity (Fire)	*yin* (寅), *wu* (午), *xu* (戌), *bing* (丙), *ding* (丁)

For the Earth Stars, there are two differing views:

Wandering Star	Most active years, months	
tian yi Hugh Door (Earth) *huo hai* Rewards (Earth)	either:	*chen* (辰), *xu* (戌), *chou* (丑), *wei* (未), *wu* (戊), *ji* (己)
	or:	*yin* (寅), *wu* (午), *xu* (戌)

"Bright Mirror" even contradicted itself in respect of the Earth Stars. In one part of the text, it says the 4 Earth Branches, meaning *chen, xu, chou, wei*; but in another part, it says *shen, zi, chen*. I believe the latter is a transcription error, which is not uncommon with old texts.

Appendix-2: "Star-Palace Interaction"

Conclusions

The reference list is by no means exhaustive, but I would think sufficient for us to form what the legal fraternity would call "a considered opinion".

The purists could well choose to follow the classics closely and disregard modern views that are ultra vires the old texts, for after all, are we not practicing classical *fengshui*? ☺ My preferred approach is to take into account all views and evaluate them on a scale of logic and reasonableness, even though such a scale is invariably subjective to an extent.

Taking stock of what we have thus far, I would table the following inferences which appear logical and reasonable, at least to me:

1. The positive Stars are strong if they are in Palaces of growth and support. Other than Bai He Ming, the other writers do not differentiate between Palace growing Star and Star growing Palace. They use the term "mutual growth" (相生), i.e. positive both ways. Hence I would disregard the issue of resource depletion in this context. Support means both Palace and Star have the same element.

2. As to which is more onerous: Palace countering Star, or Star countering Palace, classical opinion is divided almost equally. Actually this question is only of academic interest. In practical terms, when a Star is fighting the palace, whether aggressively or in defence, its ability to deliver its benevolence (in the case of a positive Star) is impaired. Like "mutual growth" described above, it is now a case of "mutual counter" (相剋).

   [Readers familiar with *xuan kong*'s static charts for the 8 house sittings (八宅生旺圖) will know that Star (visitor) countering Palace (host) is deemed more negative than Palace countering Star. But in that discussion, the reference point is the Palace and not the Star. Traditional thinking considered it abhorrent for the visitor to attack the host, and less so for the host to be hostile to the visitor.]

3. Simple as it may sound, the concept that positive Stars can never become negative, and vice versa, is in fact quite profound.

   The classics only mention positive and negative (吉凶), implying that what is not positive is automatically negative. However, the laws of physics tell us that if a positively charged particle loses its positive charge, it becomes discharged, i.e. neutral. It does not take on a negative charge. For all their brilliance, the ancient Chinese did not invent the zero in mathematics, a discrete entity in between positive and negative numbers. (The all-important zero was a Middle Eastern import.) Perhaps that explains the rather intransigent mind set of the classical writers.

   If we follow through this line of logic, a positive Star if countered will be incapacitated partially or totally, but it should not turn negative.

4. The classics do not say much about the negative Stars in this respect. Modern writers are divided on the question of whether a negative Star will behave better, or worse, when it is grown or supported by the Palace. (Like the positive Stars, we would not differentiate between growing and being grown.)

   In the old days, perhaps the question was of little practical significance as the important living quarters were not located in the negative Palaces. Maybe that's why the classics ignored it. In a modern house, it is not uncommon to find an important room at a negative Star location. So the question becomes relevant.

   Drawing on the principles of Purple Star destiny analysis, a negative Star entering a harmonious Palace (mutual growth or support) is likely to behave less negatively, the rationale being that the Star is placated in its comfort zone. But of course it is still negative by nature and will not turn positive.

5. Conversely, a negative Star being countered will turn even more malicious, not unlike a hoodlum showing his ugly side when ruffled or challenged. That is also in line with Purple Star principles.

   As to whether Palace countering negative Star is more onerous than the other way around, it hardly matters. Bad is bad enough.

6. The view that only opposite polarities between Palace and Star will invoke elemental interplay is, to my mind, inadequately substantiated. I won't buy it yet.

   It is interesting the 2 authors who mentioned "Palace and Star walking the same path" come from Taiwan. Perhaps this calls for more research using Taiwanese material.

7. The classics go to some length in describing the individual family members who will be impacted by the arrival of certain Stars at certain Palaces, such as:

   – Greedy Wolf affects the eldest son, positively when the Star is strong, negatively when it is countered;

   – Hugh Door affects the middle son;

   – Military Arts affects the youngest son;

   – Broken Soldier and Chastity harm the eldest son;

   – Literary Arts harms the middle son;

   – Rewards harms the youngest son;

   – A Star countering a Palace, or Palace countering the Star, will harm the family member associated with the Palace (*qian* = father, *kun* = mother, etc.).

Appendix-2: "Star-Palace Interaction"

In interpreting a chart, do bear in mind that the chart merely indicates the potential for an event to happen. For the event to materialize, external features ("*luan tou*", 巒頭) must support it.

Moreover, old texts tend to be alarmist in character. I would take the predictions of death and doom with a pinch of salt.

8. The analysis also provides the expected timing of an event. The Wood, Fire, Metal and Water Stars are most active during the years and months associated with the respective elements (3-Harmonies Branches, also the Stems). There is a controversy over the Earth Stars. I'm inclined to go along with the Earth frame Branches (*chen*, *xu*, *chou*, *wei*) and the Earth Stems (*wu*, *ji*).

Epilogue

Elemental interplay between Palace and Star is a useful analytical tool in advanced level 8-Mansions *fengshui*. 8-Mansions is often labeled as inadequate or old fashioned compared with newer techniques. That is grossly unfair. This time tested technique has many hidden jewels if only one cares to look for them.

from the ramblings of one hhc, a fengshui crazee
first published Aug-2006

Appendix-3:
"Swinging Hexagrams"

Appendix-3
"Swinging Hexagrams"

First there is a connection between the 8 Trigrams and the 9 "Purple White" Stars. This is defined by superimposing the *luo shu* onto the Later Heaven arrangement of the 8 Trigrams, as illustrated in Fig-A301 hereunder:

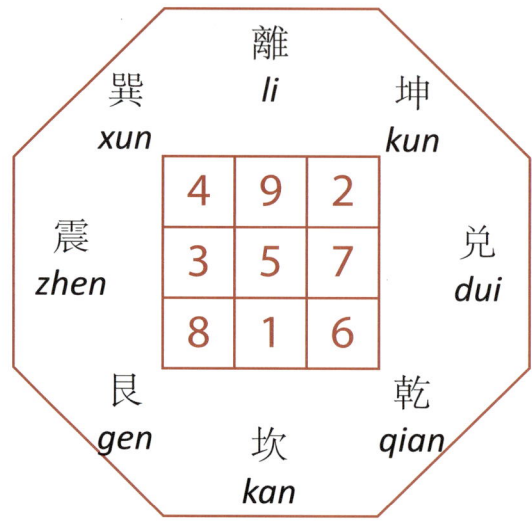

Fig-A301: Stars & Trigrams

Note that Star-5 has no Trigram associated with it.

Next we are aware a Hexagram is made up of 2 Trigrams, one stacked on top of the other. For example, the Hexagram "Unity (泰)" ☷/☰ Earth over Heaven is made up of *kun* on top of *qian*; and the Hexagram "Fellowship (同人)" ☰/☲ Heaven over Fire is made up of *qian* on top of *li*.

Now it stands to reason that a conjunction of 2 Stars can also be expressed as a Hexagram, except we may have a problem with Star-5, which we shall deal with shortly.

Appendix-3: "Swinging Hexagrams"

The technique of expressing 2 Stars in the form of a Hexagram, and the converse of that, i.e. extracting a conjunction of 2 Stars out of a given Hexagram, is called "Swinging out a Hexagram (盪卦)".

Take for example the conjunction 1-2. The "host" is Star-1 which is associated with the Trigram *kan*. The "guest" is Star-2 associated with the Trigram *kun*.

By convention, it is agreed that the "host" Trigram shall be placed at the bottom, and the "guest" on top. Hence the resultant Hexagram becomes ☷ Earth over ☵ Water, which goes by the name of "Officer (師)".

If the Star conjunction is 2-1, then kun is placed at the bottom, and kan above it. The Hexagram becomes ☵ Water over ☷ Earth, called "Alliance (比)".

In terms of Hexagram interpretation, "Officer (師)" and "Alliance (比)" are totally different, but in terms of Star conjunctions, the difference is not so big.

To the perfectionist, the difference between 1-2 and 2-1 is Earth coming to Water in the former, and Water coming to Earth in the latter. But that's like splitting hairs. In the *xuan kong* poems we are currently studying, the difference, if any, is largely ignored.

That's really it. Quite straightforward.

The only fly-in-the-ointment is Star-5 which has no Trigram associated with it. So how do we swing out a Hexagram for, say, 5-9?

xuan kong overcomes this difficult with the following workaround routine:

> In any Period other than Period-5, the Star-5 in any conjunction being contemplated is replaced by the Period Star at the centre of the "Heaven Plate", i.e. the governing Period Star.
>
> In other words, in a Period-7 chart, any Star-5 in a given conjunction will be replaced by Star-7; if Period-8 chart, by Star-8; and so on.

5-9 in a Period-7 chart would be replaced by 7-9, and the resultant Hexagram would be ☲ Fire over ☱ Marsh, called "Oppose (睽)"; and 5-9 in a Period-8 chart would be replaced by 8-9, resulting in the Hexagram "Travel (旅)" ☲ Fire over ☶ Mountain.

Appendix-3: "Swinging Hexagrams"

➢ In Period-5, the Star-5 in any conjunction being contemplated is replaced by the corresponding Star at the central palace. This is best explained by way of an example:

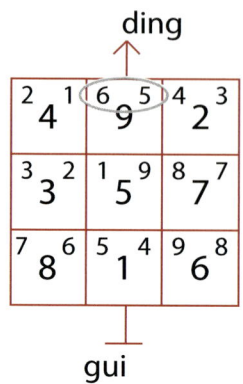

Fig-A302: Period-5

Take the case of a Period-5 property Sitting *gui* Facing *ding* (Fig-A302). The Facing palace has the conjunction 6-5. If we wish to swing out a Hexagram from this conjunction, we would replace Facing Star-5 with Star-9, which is the Facing Star at the central palace.

6-5 then becomes 6-9, which swings out the Hexagram "Great Reward (大有)" Fire over Heaven.

Of course the process is not completely reversible. If we started with the Hexagram "Great Reward (大有)" and proceeded to find its equivalent Star conjunction, we would always come up with 6-9, never 5-9. After all, the workaround routine for Star-5 is just that, some arbitrary rules to get rid of the inconvenient 5.

Appendix-3: "Swinging Hexagrams"

The following table lists the 64 Hexagrams and the Star conjunction extracted out of each Hexagram:

Hexagram name		Description	Star conjunction
Heaven	乾	Heaven over Heaven	6-6
Eliminate	夬	Marsh over Heaven	6-7
Great Reward	大有	Fire over Heaven	6-9
Great Strength	大壯	Thunder over Heaven	6-3
Small Livestock	小畜	Wind over Heaven	6-4
Waiting	需	Water over Heaven	6-1
Big Livestock	大畜	Mountain over Heaven	6-8
Unity	泰	Earth over Heaven	6-2
Tread	履	Heaven over Marsh	7-6
Marsh	兌	Marsh over Marsh	7-7
Oppose	睽	Fire over Marsh	7-9
Marrying Maiden	歸妹	Thunder over Marsh	7-3
Sincere	中孚	Wind over Marsh	7-4
Regulate	節	Water over Marsh	7-1
Decrease	損	Mountain over Marsh	7-8
Arrive	臨	Earth over Marsh	7-2
Fellowship	同人	Heaven over Fire	9-6
Reform	革	Marsh over Fire	9-7
Fire	離	Fire over Fire	9-9
Abundance	豐	Thunder over Fire	9-3
Family	家人	Wind over Fire	9-4
Accomplished	既濟	Water over Fire	9-1
Beauty	賁	Mountain over Fire	9-8
Dim Light	明夷	Earth over Fire	9-2
Without Wrongdoing	無妄	Heaven over Thunder	3-6
Follow	隨	Marsh over Thunder	3-7
Biting	噬嗑	Fire over Thunder	3-9
Thunder	震	Thunder over Thunder	3-3
Increase	益	Wind over Thunder	3-4
Begin	屯	Water over Thunder	3-1
Nourish	頤	Mountain over Thunder	3-8
Return	復	Earth over Thunder	3-2

149

Appendix-3: "Swinging Hexagrams"

Hexagram name		Description	Star conjunction
Meeting	姤	Heaven over Wind	4-6
Greater Exceed	大過	Marsh over Wind	4-7
Cauldron	鼎	Fire over Wind	4-9
Consistency	恆	Thunder over Wind	4-3
Wind	巽	Wind over Wind	4-4
Well	井	Water over Wind	4-1
Poison	蠱	Mountain over Wind	4-8
Rising	升	Earth over Wind	4-2
Litigation	訟	Heaven over Water	1-6
Trapped	困	Marsh over Water	1-7
Not Accomplished	未濟	Fire over Water	1-9
Relief	解	Thunder over Water	1-3
Disperse	渙	Wind over Water	1-4
Water	坎	Water over Water	1-1
Bliss	蒙	Mountain over Water	1-8
Officer	師	Earth over Water	1-2
Retreat	遯	Heaven over Mountain	8-6
Influence	咸	Marsh over Mountain	8-7
Travel	旅	Fire over Mountain	8-9
Lesser Exceed	小過	Thunder over Mountain	8-3
Gradual Progress	漸	Wind over Mountain	8-4
Obstruction	蹇	Water over Mountain	8-1
Mountain	艮	Mountain over Mountain	8-8
Humility	謙	Earth over Mountain	8-2
Stagnation	否	Heaven over Earth	2-6
Gathering	萃	Marsh over Earth	2-7
Advance	晉	Fire over Earth	2-9
Delight	豫	Thunder over Earth	2-3
Observation	觀	Wind over Earth	2-4
Alliance	比	Water over Earth	2-1
Peel	剝	Mountain over Earth	2-8
Earth	坤	Earth over Earth	2-2

Bibliography

Shen Zu Mian (沈祖綿)　　沈氏玄空學 (1925)
Shen Zu Mian (沈祖綿)　　玄空古義四種通釋 (1940)
Kong Zhao Su (孔昭蘇)　　孔氏玄空寶鑑 (circa 1945)
Bai He Ming (白鶴鳴)　　玄機賦飛星賦精解 (1995)
Ke Jian Cheng (柯建成)　　玄空指妙 (1997)
Zhao Xuan (趙玄)

http://www.fengshui-chinese.com/discuz/viewthread.php?tid=77244 (2011)

About the Author

Hung Hin Cheong (孔憲章) was born in 1946 at Kuala Lumpur, Malaysia. He received his early education in Malaysia before continuing with his tertiary education in the United Kingdom. He graduated with a Bachelor of Science degree with honours (1st class) in electrical and electronic engineering from the University of Leeds, England, in 1969.

He built his career in the electrical industry, and held the position of Chief Executive at a large international electrical equipment manufacturer, before his retirement in 2001.

fengshui has been the author's passion for many years. He studied under several masters over the years, and was appointed an instructor with the Mastery Academy of Chinese Metaphysics founded by Master Joey Yap, teaching *fengshui* and date selection since 2006.

The author was privileged to be schooled in both English and Chinese from a young age. This provided him access to the wide spectrum of *fengshui* material available in Chinese, which he perused avidly, ranging from ancient classics to popular magazines. This, together with his upbringing in a family steeped in Chinese traditions, afforded him a rare insight into the cultural background of classical *fengshui*. This advantage and his bilingual competence put him in good stead to help propagate classical *fengshui* knowledge to the wider world.

The author's engineering training also enabled him to put abstract and often ambiguous metaphysical concepts into a structured, logical and practical framework. He has published a number of papers in the electronic medium, which demonstrated his skill in translating and explaining classical texts clearly and succinctly in his own inimitable style. They also showed he was not shy of speaking his own mind when certain old ideas were clearly inconsistent with modern realities.

His first book, the "*xuan kong* Purple White Script (玄空紫白訣)" published in 2009, was well received by the English speaking *fengshui* community. This was followed by the second book "Secrets of *xuan kong* (玄空秘旨)" in 2011, and now a third book that examines yet another of the "4 Celebrated Poems of *xuan kong* (玄空四大名賦)".

In this book, the poem "Ode to Mysticism (玄機賦)" is placed under the same degree of critical scrutiny as in the previous cases, which amply demonstrates the author's unwavering commitment to bringing classical *fengshui* texts out of the closet into the wider *fengshui* world.

Further Your Xuan Kong Knowledge
Recommended Courses

Xuan Kong Mastery Module 2B: Xuan Kong Purple White Feng Shui

Purple White is a fundamental course that is essential to your understanding of Xuan Kong Purple White. Be guided by Joey Yap on the treasured secrets of the Purple White Script. Discover a powerful and vibrant form of Xuan Kong. It will transform the way you approach and practice Xuan Kong Feng Shui.

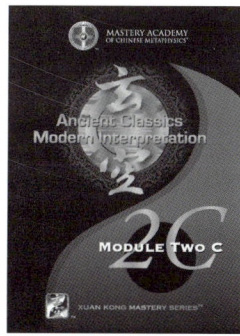

Xuan Kong Mastery Module 2C: Ancient Classics Modern Interpretation

Focusing on decoding the secrets of the **Xuan Ji Fu** 玄機賦 or **Ode to Mysticism**, one of the four classic texts of Xuan Kong, particularly famous for its secrets to the Xuan Kong Life Palace divination technique. It also carries the hidden code to unlock a deeper side of Eight Mansions Feng Shui, and the secret to understanding the many Xuan Kong Hexagram combinations that allow the practitioner to, in many cases - predict outcomes and foresee the future. The secrets in this classic will allow you to penetrate a much, much deeper level of mastery in Xuan Kong Feng Shui.

www.masteryacademy.com /purplewhite

MASTERY ACADEMY OF CHINESE METAPHYSICS
Your **Preferred** Choice to the Art & Science of Classical Chinese Metaphysics Studies

Bringing **innovative** techniques
and **creative** teaching methods
to an ancient study.

Mastery Academy of Chinese Metaphysics was established by Joey Yap to play the role of disseminating this Eastern knowledge to the modern world with the belief that this valuable knowledge should be accessible to anyone, anywhere.

Its goal is to enrich people's lives through accurate, professional teaching and practice of Chinese Metaphysics knowledge globally. It is the first academic institution of its kind in the world to adopt the tradition of Western institutions of higher learning - where students are encourage to explore, question and challenge themselves and to respect different fields and branches of study - with the appreciation and respect of classical ideas and applications that have stood the test of time.

The art and science of Chinese Metaphysics studies – be it Feng Shui, BaZi (Astrology), Mian Xiang (Face Reading), ZeRi (Date Selection) or Yi Jing – is no longer a field shrouded with mystery and superstition. In light of new technology, fresher interpretations and innovative methods as well as modern teaching tools like the Internet, interactive learning, e-learning and distance learning, anyone from virtually any corner of the globe, who is keen to master these disciplines can do so with ease and confidence under the guidance and support of the Academy.

It has indeed proven to be a center of educational excellence for thousands of students from over thirty countries across the world; many of whom have moved on to practice classical Chinese Metaphysics professionally in their home countries.

At the Academy, we believe in enriching people's lives by empowering their destinies through the disciplines of Chinese Metaphysics. Learning is not an option - it's a way of life!

MALAYSIA
19-3, The Boulevard, Mid Valley City, 59200 Kuala Lumpur, Malaysia
Tel : +603-2284 8080 | Fax : +603-2284 1218
Email   : info@masteryacademy.com
Website : www.masteryacademy.com

Australia, Austria, Canada, China, Croatia, Cyprus, Czech Republic, Denmark, France, Germany, Greece, Hungary, India, Italy, Kazakhstan, Malaysia, Netherlands (Holland), New Zealand, Philippines, Poland, Russian Federation, Singapore, Slovenia, South Africa, Switzerland, Turkey, U.S.A., Ukraine, United Kingdom

www.masteryacademy.com | +603 - 2284 8080

JOEY YAP CONSULTING GROUP

Pioneering Metaphysics - Centric Personal Coaching and Corporate Consulting

The Joey Yap Consulting Group is the world's first specialised metaphysics consultation firm. Founded in 2002 by renown international Feng Shui and BaZi consultant, author and trainer Joey Yap, the Joey Yap Consulting Group is a pioneer in the provision of metaphysics-driven coaching and consultation services for individuals and corporations.

The Group's core consultation practice areas are Feng Shui and BaZi, which are complimented by ancillary services like Date Selection, Face Reading and Yi Jing Divination. The Group's team of highly-trained professional consultants are led by Principal Consultant Joey Yap. The Joey Yap Consulting Group is the firm of choice for corporate captains, entrepreneurs, celebrities and property developers when it comes to Feng Shui and BaZi-related advisory and knowledge.

Across Industries: Our Portfolio of Clients

Our diverse portfolio of both corporate and individual clients from all around the world bears testimony to our experience and capabilities.

Joey Yap Consulting Group is the firm of choice for many of Asia's leading multi-national corporations, listed entities, conglomerates and top-tier property developers when it comes to Feng Shui and corporate BaZi.

Our services also engaged by professionals, prominent business personalities, celebrities, high-profile politicians and people from all walks of life.

JOEY YAP CONSULTING GROUP

Name (Mr./Mrs./Ms.):_____

Contact Details

Tel:_____ Fax:_____

Mobile :_____

E-mail:_____

What Type of Consultation Are You Interested In?
☐ Feng Shui   ☐ BaZi   ☐ Date Selection   ☐ Corporate Events

Please tick if applicable:
☐ Are you a Property Developer looking to engage Joey Yap Consulting Group?
☐ Are you a Property Investor looking for tailor-made packages to suit your investment requirements?

Please attach your name card here.

Thank you for completing this form. Please fax it back to us at:

Malaysia & the rest of the world
Fax : +603-2284 2213   Tel : +603-2284 1213

www.joeyyap.com

www.joeyyap.com

Feng Shui Consultations

For Residential Properties
- Initial Land/Property Assessment
- Residential Feng Shui Consultations
- Residential Land Selection
- End-to-End Residential Consultation

For Commercial Properties
- Initial Land/Property Assessment
- Commercial Feng Shui Consultations
- Commercial Land Selection
- End-to-End Commercial Consultation

For Property Developers
- End-to-End Consultation
- Post-Consultation Advisory Services
- Panel Feng Shui Consultant

For Property Investors
- Your Personal Feng Shui Consultant
- Tailor-Made Packages

For Memorial Parks & Burial Sites
- Yin House Feng Shui

BaZi Consultations

Personal Destiny Analysis
- Personal Destiny Analysis for Individuals
- Children's BaZi Analysis
- Family BaZi Analysis

Strategic Analysis for Corporate Organizations
- Corporate BaZi Consultations
- BaZi Analysis for Human Resource Management

Entrepreneurs & Business Owners
- BaZi Analysis for Entrepreneurs

Career Pursuits
- BaZi Career Analysis

Relationships
- Marriage and Compatibility Analysis
- Partnership Analysis

For Everyone
- Annual BaZi Forecast
- Your Personal BaZi Coach

Date Selection Consultations

- **Marriage Date Selection**
- **Caesarean Birth Date Selection**
- **House-Moving Date Selection**
- **Renovation & Groundbreaking Dates**

- **Signing of Contracts**
- **Official Openings**
- **Product Launches**

Corporate Events

Many reputable organizations and instituitions have worked closely with Joey Yap Consulting Group to build a synergistic business relationship by engaging our team of consultants, led by Joey Yap, as speakers at their corporate events.

We tailor our seminars and talks to suit the anticipated or pertinent group of audience. Be it department, subsidiary, your clients or even the entire corporation, we aim to fit your requirements in delivering the intended message(s).

Tel: +603-2284 1213   Email: consultation@joeyyap.com

CHINESE METAPHYSICS REFERENCE SERIES

The Chinese Metaphysics Reference Series is a collection of reference texts, source material, and educational textbooks to be used as supplementary guides by scholars, students, researchers, teachers and practitioners of Chinese Metaphysics.

These comprehensive and structured books provide fast, easy reference to aid in the study and practice of various Chinese Metaphysics subjects including Feng Shui, BaZi, Yi Jing, Zi Wei, Liu Ren, Ze Ri, Ta Yi, Qi Men and Mian Xiang.

The Chinese Metaphysics Compendium

At over 1,000 pages, the *Chinese Metaphysics Compendium* is a unique one-volume reference book that compiles all the formulas relating to Feng Shui, BaZi (Four Pillars of Destiny), Zi Wei (Purple Star Astrology), Yi Jing (I-Ching), Qi Men (Mystical Doorways), Ze Ri (Date Selection), Mian Xiang (Face Reading) and other sources of Chinese Metaphysics.

It is presented in the form of easy-to-read tables, diagrams and reference charts, all of which are compiled into one handy book. This first-of-its-kind compendium is presented in both English and the original Chinese, so that none of the meanings and contexts of the technical terminologies are lost.

The only essential and comprehensive reference on Chinese Metaphysics, and an absolute must-have for all students, scholars, and practitioners of Chinese Metaphysics.

The Ten Thousand Year Calendar (Pocket Edition)

The Ten Thousand Year Calendar

Dong Gong Date Selection

The Date Selection Compendium

Plum Blossoms Divination Reference Book

San Yuan Dragon Gate Eight Formations Water Method

Xuan Kong Da Gua Ten Thousand Year Calendar

Bazi Hour Pillar Useful Gods - Wood

Bazi Hour Pillar Useful Gods - Fire

Bazi Hour Pillar Useful Gods - Earth

Bazi Hour Pillar Useful Gods - Metal

Bazi Hour Pillar Useful Gods - Water

Xuan Kong Da Gua Structures Reference Book

Xuan Kong Da Gua 64 Gua Transformation Analysis

Bazi Structures and Structural Useful Gods - Wood

Bazi Structures and Structural Useful Gods - Fire

Bazi Structures and Structural Useful Gods - Earth

Bazi Structures and Structural Useful Gods - Metal

Bazi Structures and Structural Useful Gods - Water

Xuan Kong Purple White Script

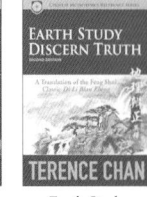
Earth Study Discern Truth Second Edition

www.masteryacademy.com | +603 - 2284 8080

Joey Yap's BaZi Profiling System

Three Levels of BaZi Profiling (English & Chinese versions)

In BaZi Profiling, there are three levels that reflect three different stages of a person's personal nature and character structure.

Level 1 – The Day Master

The Day Master in a nutshell is the BASIC YOU. The inborn personality. It is your essential character. It answers the basic question "WHO AM I". There are ten basic personality profiles – the TEN Day Masters – each with its unique set of personality traits, likes and dislikes.

Level 2 – The Structure

The Structure is your behavior and attitude – in other words, how you use your personality. It expands on the Day Master (Level 1). The structure reveals your natural tendencies in life – are you more controlling, more of a creator, supporter, thinker or connector? Each of the Ten Day Masters express themselves differently through the FIVE Structures. Why do we do the things we do? Why do we like the things we like? – The answers are in our BaZi STRUCTURE.

Level 3 – The Profile

The Profile reveals your unique abilities and skills, the masks that you consciously and unconsciously "put on" as you approach and navigate the world. Your Profile speaks of your ROLES in life. There are TEN roles – or Ten BaZi Profiles. Everyone plays a different role.

What makes you happy and what does success mean to you is different to somebody else. Your sense of achievement and sense of purpose in life is unique to your Profile. Your Profile will reveal your unique style.

The path of least resistance to your success and wealth can only be accessed once you get into your "flow." Your BaZi Profile reveals how you can get FLOW. It will show you your patterns in work, relationship and social settings. Being AWARE of these patterns is your first step to positive Life Transformation.

www.baziprofiling.com

BaZi Collections

Leading Chinese Astrology Master Trainer Joey Yap makes it easy to learn how to unlock your Destiny through your BaZi with these books. BaZi or Four Pillars of Destiny is an ancient Chinese science which enables individuals to understand their personality, hidden talents and abilities as well as their luck cycle, simply by examining the information contained within their birth data.

Understand and appreciate more about this astoundingly accurate ancient Chinese Metaphysical science with this BaZi Collection.

Feng Shui Collection

Must-Haves for Property Analysis!

For homeowners, those looking to build their own home or even investors who are looking to apply Feng Shui to their homes, these series of books provides valuable information from the classical Feng Shui therioes and applications.

In his trademark straight-to-the-point manner, Joey shares with you the Feng Shui do's and dont's when it comes to finding a property with favorable Feng Shui, which is condusive for home living.

Stories & Lessons on Feng Shui Series

All in all, this series is a delightful chronicle of Joey's articles, thoughts and vast experience - as a professional Feng Shui consultant and instructor - that have been purposely refined, edited and expanded upon to make for a light-hearted, interesting yet educational read. And with Feng Shui, BaZi, Mian Xiang and Yi Jing all thrown into this one dish, there's something for everyone.

www.masteryacademy.com | +603 - 2284 8080

Continue Your Journey with Joey Yap Books in Feng Shui

Pure Feng Shui

Pure Feng Shui is Joey Yap's debut with an international publisher, CICO Books, and is a refreshing and elegant look at the intricacies of Classical Feng Shui – now compiled in a useful manner for modern-day readers. This book is a comprehensive introduction to all the important precepts and techniques of Feng Shui practice.

Your Aquarium Here

This book is the first in Fengshuilogy Series, a series of matter-in-fact and useful Feng Shui books designed for the person who wants to do a fuss-free Feng Shui.

Xuan Kong Flying Stars

This book is an essential introductory book to the subject of Xuan Kong Fei Xing, a well-known and popular system of Feng Shui. Learn 'tricks of the trade' and 'trade secrets' to enhance and maximize Qi in your home or office.

Walking the Dragons

Compiled in one book for the first time from Joey Yap's Feng Shui Mastery Excursion Series, the book highlights China's extensive, vibrant history with astute observations on the Feng Shui of important sites and places. Learn the landform formations of Yin Houses (tombs and burial places), as well as mountains, temples, castles, and villages.

The Art of Date Selection: Personal Date Selection

With the *Art of Date Selection: Personal Date Selection*, learn simple, practical methods you can employ to select not just good dates, but personalized good dates. Whether it's a personal activity such as a marriage or professional endeavor such as launching a business, signing a contract or even acquiring assets, this book will show you how to pick the good dates and tailor them to suit the activity in question, as well as avoid the negative ones too!

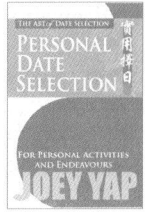

www.masteryacademy.com | +603 - 2284 8080

Face Reading Collection

Discover Face Reding (English & Chinese versions)

This is a comprehensive book on all areas of Face Reading, covering some of the most important facial features, including the forehead, mouth, ears and even philtrum above your lips. This book eill help you analyse not just your Destiny but help you achieve your full potential and achieve life fulfillment.

Joey Yap's Art of Face Reading

The Art of Face Reading is Joey Yap's second effort with CICO Books, and takes a lighter, more practical approach to Face Reading. This book does not so much focus on the individual features as it does on reading the entire face. It is about identifying common personality types and characters.

Easy Guide on Face Reading (English & Chinese versions)

The Face Reading Essentials series of books comprises 5 individual books on the key features of the face – Eyes, Eyebrows, Ears, Nose, and Mouth. Each book provides a detailed illustration and a simple yet descriptive explanation on the individual types of the features.

The books are equally useful and effective for beginners, enthusiasts, and the curious. The series is designed to enable people who are new to Face Reading to make the most of first impressions and learn to apply Face Reading skills to understand the personality and character of friends, family, co-workers, and even business associates.

Annual Releases

2011 Annual Outlook & Tong Shu

Chinese Astrology for 2011 | Feng Shui for 2011 | Tong Shu Desktop Calendar 2011 | Professional Tong Shu Diary 2011 | Tong Shu Monthly Planner 2011 | Weekly Tong Shu Diary 2011

Educational Tools and Software

Xuan Kong Flying Stars Feng Shui Software
The Essential Application for Enthusiasts and Professionals

The Xuan Kong Flying Stars Feng Shui Software will assist you in the practice of Xuan Kong Feng Shui with minimum fuss and maximum effectiveness. Superimpose the Flying Stars charts over your house plans (or those of your clients) to clearly demarcate the 9 Palaces. Use it to help you create fast and sophisticated chart drawings and presentations, as well as to assist professional practitioners in the report-writing process before presenting the final reports for your clients. Students can use it to practice their Xuan Kong Feng Shui skills and knowledge, and it can even be used by designers and architects!

BaZi Ming Pan Software Version 2.0
Professional Four Pillars Calculator for Destiny Analysis

The BaZi Ming Pan Version 2.0 Professional Four Pillars Calculator for Destiny Analysis is the most technically advanced software of its kind in the world today. It allows even those without any knowledge of BaZi to generate their own BaZi Charts, and provides virtually every detail required to undertake a comprehensive Destiny Analysis.

This Professional Four Pillars Calculator allows you to even undertake a day-to-day analysis of your Destiny. What's more, all BaZi Charts generated by this software are fully printable and configurable! Designed for both enthusiasts and professional practitioners, this state-of-the-art software blends details with simplicity, and is capable of generating 4 different types of BaZi charts: **BaZi Professional Charts, BaZi Annual Analysis Charts, BaZi Pillar Analysis Charts and BaZi Family Relationship Charts.**

Joey Yap Feng Shui Template Set

Directions are the cornerstone of any successful Feng Shui audit or application. The **Joey Yap Feng Shui Template Set** is a set of three templates to simplify the process of taking directions and determining locations and positions, whether it's for a building, a house, or an open area such as a plot of land, all with just a floor plan or area map.

The Set comprises 3 basic templates: The Basic Feng Shui Template, 8 Mansions Feng Shui Template, and the Flying Stars Feng Shui Template.

Mini Feng Shui Compass

The Mini Feng Shui Compass is a self-aligning compass that is not only light at 100gms but also built sturdily to ensure it will be convenient to use anywhere. The rings on the Mini Feng Shui Compass are bi-lingual and incorporate the 24 Mountain Rings that is used in your traditional Luo Pan.

The comprehensive booklet included will guide you in applying the 24 Mountain Directions on your Mini Feng Shui Compass effectively and the 8 Mansions Feng Shui to locate the most auspicious locations within your home, office and surroundings. You can also use the Mini Feng Shui Compass when measuring the direction of your property for the purpose of applying Flying Stars Feng Shui.

www.masteryacademy.com | +603 - 2284 8080

Educational Tools and Software

Xuan Kong Vol.1
An Advanced Feng Shui Home Study Course

Learn the Xuan Kong Flying Star Feng Shui system in just 20 lessons! Joey Yap's specialised notes and course work have been written to enable distance learning without compromising on the breadth or quality of the syllabus. Learn at your own pace with the same material students in a live class would use. The most comprehensive distance learning course on Xuan Kong Flying Star Feng Shui in the market. Xuan Kong Flying Star Vol.1 comes complete with a special binder for all your course notes.

Feng Shui for Period 8 - (DVD)

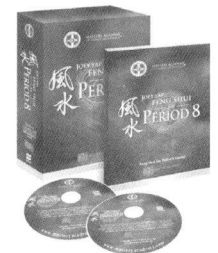

Don't miss the Feng Shui Event of the next 20 years! Catch Joey Yap LIVE and find out just what Period 8 is all about. This DVD boxed set zips you through the fundamentals of Feng Shui and the impact of this important change in the Feng Shui calendar. Joey's entertaining, conversational style walks you through the key changes that Period 8 will bring and how to tap into Wealth Qi and Good Feng Shui for the next 20 years.

Xuan Kong Flying Stars Beginners Workshop - (DVD)

Take a front row seat in Joey Yap's Xuan Kong Flying Stars workshop with this unique LIVE RECORDING of Joey Yap's Xuan Kong Flying Stars Feng Shui workshop, attended by over 500 people. This DVD program provides an effective and quick introduction of Xuan Kong Feng Shui essentials for those who are just starting out in their study of classical Feng Shui. Learn to plot your own Flying Star chart in just 3 hours. Learn 'trade secret' methods, remedies and cures for Flying Stars Feng Shui. This boxed set contains 3 DVDs and 1 workbook with notes and charts for reference.

BaZi Four Pillars of Destiny Beginners Workshop - (DVD)

Ever wondered what Destiny has in store for you? Or curious to know how you can learn more about your personality and inner talents? BaZi or Four Pillars of Destiny is an ancient Chinese science that enables us to understand a person's hidden talent, inner potential, personality, health and wealth luck from just their birth data. This specially compiled DVD set of Joey Yap's BaZi Beginners Workshop provides a thorough and comprehensive introduction to BaZi. Learn how to read your own chart and understand your own luck cycle. This boxed set contains 3 DVDs and 1 workbook with notes and reference charts.

www.masteryacademy.com | +603 - 2284 8080

DVD Series

Joey Yap's Face Reading Revealed DVD Series

Mian Xiang, the Chinese art of Face Reading, is an ancient form of physiognomy and entails the use of the face and facial characteristics to evaluate key aspects of a person's life, luck and destiny. In his Face Reading DVDs series, Joey Yap shows you how the facial features reveal a wealth of information about a person's luck, destiny and personality.

Mian Xiang also tell us the talents, quirks and personality of an individual. Do you know that just by looking at a person's face, you can ascertain his or her health, wealth, relationships and career? Let Joey Yap show you how the 12 Palaces can be utilised to reveal a person's inner talents, characteristics and much more.

Feng Shui for Homebuyers DVD Series

In these DVDs, you will also learn how to identify properties with good Feng Shui features that will help you promote a fulfilling life and achieve your full potential. Discover how to avoid properties with negative Feng Shui that can bring about detrimental effects to your health, wealth and relationships.

Joey will also elaborate on how to fix the various aspects of your home that may have an impact on the Feng Shui of your property and give pointers on how to tap into the positive energies to support your goals.

Discover Feng Shui with Joey Yap: Set of 4 DVDs
Informative and entertaining, classical Feng Shui comes alive in *Discover Feng Shui with Joey Yap!*

You have the questions. Now let Joey personally answer them in this 4-set DVD compilation! Learn how to ensure the viability of your residence or workplace, Feng Shui-wise, without having to convert it into a Chinese antiques' shop. Classical Feng Shui is about harnessing the natural power of your environment to improve quality of life. It's a systematic and subtle metaphysical science.

Walking the Dragons with Joey Yap (The TV Series)

This DVD set features eight episodes, covering various landform Feng Shui analyses and applications from Joey Yap as he and his co-hosts travel through China. It includes case studies of both modern and historical sites with a focus on Yin House (burial places) Feng Shui and the tombs of the Qing Dynasty emperors.

The series was partly filmed on-location in mainland China, and the state of Selangor, Malaysia.

www.masteryacademy.com | +603 - 2284 8080

Home Study Courses

Gain Valuable Knowledge from the Comfort of Your Home

Now, armed with your trusty computer or laptop and Internet access, knowledge of Chinese Metaphysics is just a click away!

3 easy steps to activate your Home Study Course:

Step 1:
Go to the URL as indicated on the Activation Card, and key in your Activation Code

Step 2:
At the Registration page, fill in the details accordingly to enable us to generate your Student Identification (Student ID).

Step 3:
Upon successful registration, you may begin your lessons immediately.

Joey Yap's Feng Shui Mastery HomeStudy Course

Module 1: **Empowering Your Home**
Module 2: **Master Practitioner Program**

Learn how easy it is to harness the power of the environment to promote health, wealth and prosperity in your life. The knowledge and applications of Feng Shui will no more be a mystery but a valuable tool you can master on your own.

Joey Yap's BaZi Mastery HomeStudy Course

Module 1: **Mapping Your Life**
Module 2: **Mastering Your Future**

Discover your path of least resistance to success with insights about your personality and capabilities, and what strengths you can tap on to maximize your potential for success and happiness by mastering BaZi (Chinese Astrology). This course will teach you all the essentials you need to interpret a BaZi chart and more.

Joey Yap's Mian Xiang Mastery HomeStudy Course

Module 1: **Face Reading**
Module 2: **Advanced Face Reading**

A face can reveal so much about a person. Now, you can learn the art and science of Mian Xiang (Chinese Face Reading) to understand a person's character based on his or her facial features with ease and confidence.

www.masteryacademy.com | +603 - 2284 8080

Feng Shui Mastery Series™
LIVE COURSES (MODULES ONE TO FOUR)

The Feng Shui Mastery Series™ comprises Feng Shui Mastery Modules 1, 2, 3 and 4. It starts off with a foundation program up to the advanced practitioner level. It is a thorough, comprehensive program that covers important theories from various classical Feng Shui systems including Ba Zhai, San Yuan, San He, and Xuan Kong.

Module One: Beginners Course **Module Two:** Practitioners Course **Module Three:** Advanced Practitioners Course **Module Four:** Master Course

BaZi Mastery Series™
LIVE COURSES (MODULES ONE TO FOUR)

The BaZi Mastery Series™ consists of BaZi Mastery Modules 1, 2, 3 and 4. In Modules 1 and 2, students will receive a thorough introduction to BaZi, along with an intensive understanding of BaZi principles and the requisite skills to practice it with accuracy and precision. This will prepare them, and serious Feng Shui practitioners, for a more advanced levels and fine-tune their application skills in Modules 3 and 4.

Module One: Intensive Foundation Course **Module Two:** Practitioners Course **Module Three:** Advanced Practitioners Course **Module Four:** Master Course in BaZi

XUAN KONG MASTERY SERIES™
LIVE COURSES (MODULES ONE TO THREE)
* Advanced Courses For Master Practitioners

The Xuan Kong Mastery Series™ comprises Xuan Kong Mastery Modules 1, 2A, 2B and 3. It is a sophisticated branch of Feng Shui replete with many techniques and formulae, enabling practitioners to evaluate Feng Shui on a more thorough and in-depth basis. The study of Xuan Kong encompasses numerology, symbology and science of the Ba Gua along with the mathematics of time.

  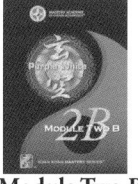 

Module One: Advanced Foundation Course **Module Two A:** Advanced Xuan Kong Methodologies **Module Two B:** Purple White **Module Three:** Advanced Xuan Kong Da Gua

www.masteryacademy.com | +603 - 2284 8080

Mian Xiang Mastery Series™
LIVE COURSES (MODULES ONE AND TWO)

The Mian Xiang Mastery Series™ comprises of Mian Xiang Mastery Modules 1 and 2 to allow students to learn this ancient art in a thorough, detailed manner. Each module has a carefully-developed syllabus that allows students to get acquainted with the fundamentals of Mian Xiang before moving on to the more intricate theories and principles that will enable them to practice Mian Xiang with greater depth and complexity.

Module One:
Basic Face Reading

Module Two:
Practical Face Reading

Yi Jing Mastery Series™
LIVE COURSES (MODULES ONE AND TWO)

The Yi Jing Mastery Series™ comprises Modules 1 and 2. Both Modules aim to give casual and serious Yi Jing enthusiasts a serious insight into one of the most important philosophical treatises in ancient Chinese thought. Yi Jing uses sophisticated formulas and calculations to derive the answers to questions we pose. It is a science of divination, and in our classes there is a heavy emphasis on the scientific aspect of it. It bears no religious or superstitious affiliation.

Module One:
Traditional Yi Jing

Module Two:
Plum Blossom Numerology

Ze Ri Mastery Series™
LIVE COURSES (MODULES ONE AND TWO)

The ZeRi Mastery Series™ consists of ZeRi Mastery Modules 1 and 2. This program provides students with a thorough introduction to the art of Date Selection both for Personal and Feng Shui purposes. Our ZeRi Mastery Series™ aims to provide a thorough and comprehensive program on the art of Date Selection, covering everything from Personal and Feng Shui Date Selection to Xuan Kong Da Gua Date Selection.

Module One:
Personal and Feng Shui Date Selection

Module Two:
Xuan Kong Da Gua Date Selection

www.masteryacademy.com | +603 - 2284 8080

Feng Shui for Life

This is an entry-level five-day course designed for the Feng Shui beginner to learn the application of practical Feng Shui in day-to-day living. Lessons include quick tips on analyzing the BaZi chart, simple Feng Shui solutions for the home, basic Date Selection, useful Face Reading techniques and practical Water formulas. A great introduction course on Chinese Metaphysics studies for beginners.

Joey Yap's
Design Your Destiny

This is a three-day life transformation program designed to inspire awareness and action for you to create a better quality of life. It introduces the DRT™ (Decision Referential Technology) method, which utilizes the BaZi Personality Profiling system to determine the right version of you, and serves as a tool to help you make better decisions and achieve a better life in the least resistant way possible based on your Personality Profile Type.

Walk the Mountains! Learn Feng Shui in a Practical and Hands-on Program

 ## Feng Shui Mastery Excursion™

Learn landform (Luan Tou) Feng Shui by walking the mountains and chasing the Dragon's vein in China. This Program takes the students in a study tour to examine notable Feng Shui landmarks, mountains, hills, valleys, ancient palaces, famous mansions, houses and tombs in China. The Excursion is a 'practical' hands-on course where students are shown to perform readings using the formulas they've learnt and to recognize and read Feng Shui Landform (Luan Tou) formations.

Read about China Excursion here:
http://www.fengshuiexcursion.com

Mastery Academy courses are conducted around the world. Find out when will Joey Yap be in your area by visiting **www.masteryacademy.com** or call our office at **+603-2284 8080**.

---

www.masteryacademy.com | +603 - 2284 8080